A MONSTER IN MOUNT PLEASANT

A STORY OF MURDERS AND JUSTICE

CJ WILLIAMS

Genius
Book Publishing

A Monster in Mount Pleasant

Copyright © 2025 CJ Williams

Published by:
Genius Book Publishing
PO Box 250380
Milwaukee Wisconsin 53225
GeniusBookPublishing.com

ISBN: 978-1-958727-61-4

250214 HQ

CONTENTS

Foreword   v

1. Murder at the Beavers'   1
2. My Hometown Murders   11
3. Mount Pleasant Then   16
4. The Beavers   26
5. Max's Disastrous Discovery   47
6. The Seagers   74
7. The Initial Investigation   97
8. "The Mood Here is Dark, Somber"   116
9. The Iris Restaurant   127
10. Susan Wheelock   140
11. Murder at the Iris   148
12. Monte Charged   162
13. Monte's Great Escape   181
14. Beavers' Murder Investigation (Continued)   201
15. Prosecution and Suppression   218
16. Round Two   229
17. Monte on Trial   248
18. The Appeal   277
19. Monte's Retrial   283
20. Epilogue   290

Acknowledgments   305

FOREWORD

In the fall of 1978, in a quiet, little Iowa town, an 18-year old high school student snuck into a house late one evening and shot a middle-aged woman in the back of the head as she sat watching T.V. Then he shot the woman's 16-year-old daughter, his classmate. As the daughter was dying of her wounds, the killer raped her. For six months, the crime went unsolved, the police lacking a suspect, or even a decent lead. Then, late one night after a restaurant bar had closed, a murderer bludgeoned to death a young waitress who had stumbled upon her killer while he was burglarizing the place. The murderer would eventually be caught, prosecuted, and convicted, but only after the passage of 22 years.

These murders, and the murderer, have haunted and intrigued me since I was 16 years old. You see, the murderer, Monte Seager, and his teenage victim, Karol Beavers, were my high school classmates. Karol's parents,

Max and Clementine, were my family's friends. And I worked with the murdered waitress, Sue Wheelock, and the murderer himself, at the restaurant where she died.

The story of these murders and the murderer are fascinating for many reasons. It involves multiple murders within a short time by a single individual with no prior history of violence. It involves the murder and rape of a popular high school girl. The murders were committed in a quiet little town largely unfamiliar with violent crime. The murderer himself was the product of a broken home, foster and group homes, and an alcoholic and blind father. The legal proceedings were long and complicated with many twists and turns. The investigation and prosecution involved a lying chief of police, hypnosis-induced testimony, the suppression of evidence, the dismissal of murder charges, an escape, a capture of the murderer halfway across the country after a high speed chase, the resurrection of murder charges, and multiple trials. Last, the murderer, serving two life terms without parole, has met with me and for the first time has confessed to the murders of my classmate and her mother. You can't make these things up.

These victims weren't important people outside their community. They weren't famous. They weren't celebrities, even in death. There are news reports of murders every day, so these murders of the distant past in some ways are no more important, deserve perhaps no more time and attention, than one devotes over breakfast when reading in the daily paper about the latest crimes.

Yet, these murders and the subsequent investigation

and prosecution of the murderer are important, even today. The horror of the events are still chilling. The psychological and social forces that converged to lead this troubled high school kid to slaughter three women in six months remain at work today on other young men. The consequences of broken homes, and failures of foster and group homes, continue to impact society today. The flaws and foibles of the criminal investigation and problem-laden prosecution are the same as those at play in many cases today. And the impact such random and pointless violence had on the family members and community continue to be repeated with each new murder today.

While the case coursed its way through the court system, I finished high school, graduated college, then law school. I became a federal prosecutor, influenced, in part, by these formative events. Now, I am a federal judge. After a career spent practicing law primarily in the criminal justice system, I finally decided to dig into this case, investigate it, and write about what I found. I wanted to try to discern why this 18-year-old high school classmate killed three people in the course of six months. The goal was to discover, if I could, what motivated him to rape and murder Karol, our popular and sweet classmate, and kill her kind and innocent mother in cold blood. What led him, I wondered, to beat a young, amiable, but troubled waitress to death. In researching and writing this book, I wanted to somehow try to comprehend, then explain, how someone could commit such monstrous acts, as the murderer's defense attorneys described them.

My journey would take several years. I have scoured

over the court files, viewed the evidence, looked at crime scene photographs, and read transcripts, autopsy reports, investigation reports and other materials (including Monte's own hand-written notes about the legal proceedings), and analyzed the criminal investigation and prosecution. My research included pouring over public records and reading countless old newspaper articles. I have also interviewed scores of people with knowledge of the murders including the victims' family members, classmates, friends, law enforcement officers, and prosecutors. I even questioned the murderer himself. In the process I discovered poignant and intriguing facts about the backgrounds of both the murderer and his victims. It helped me shed the victim label from these women to reveal them as the loving and innocent people they were. And it brought me face to face with a cold blooded murderer.

In writing this book, I have relied at times on my own memories and my personal knowledge of the key players and the town in which I grew up and where the murders occurred. I returned to my home town many times while researching this book. I have walked the path between where Monte's house once stood and the home where he slew Clementine and Karol. I timed how long it took Monte to walk that path as he did on the night of October 29, 1978. I have returned to the scenes of the crimes and other events, locations I once haunted as a child. In writing this book, I have also relied on my own education, experience, and expertise in the criminal justice system. And, perhaps most importantly, I have spent hours with

Monte Seager himself, interviewing him in a stale prison visitation room over the course of several visits.

This, then, is the story of Monte's murders, and the lives he destroyed.

ONE
MURDER AT THE BEAVERS'

"There was an iciness, a sinking, a sickening of the heart—an unredeemed dreariness of thought which no goading of the imagination could torture into aught of the sublime." – Edgar Allan Poe, THE FALL OF THE HOUSE OF USHER AND OTHER TALES

ON A COOL SATURDAY EVENING LATE IN THE MONTH of October, 1978, Max and Clementine Beavers hosted a cocktail party for several friends in their brick ranch-style home in the small Iowa town of Mount Pleasant. Earlier that day, their vivacious 16-year-old daughter, Karol, had helped her mother make hors d'oeuvres for their guests. At the party, Karol mingled with the adults, chatting with them about the upcoming Powder Puff football game in which she was going to play the following week as part of the high school's homecoming events. Everyone was in a happy mood that pleasant evening.

At one point during the cocktail party, Max escorted

the other couples to the basement to show off the new rust, brown, and gold-colored shag carpeting that workers had just installed in the den that Friday. The new carpet was a gift from Max to Clementine for their 35th wedding anniversary, he explained to his guests. Clementine had been wanting new carpet for quite some time. At Clementine's request, Max had the stairs to the basement carpeted as well; now they didn't squeak nearly as much as they used to.

After the cocktail party, the adults drove to the Mount Pleasant Country Club on the west side of town to attend an Octoberfest party. Meanwhile, Karol went out for the evening with some of her high school friends. A little before 11:00 p.m., Max and Clementine left the party at the country club and returned home. By the time they arrived home, Karol was already there, in her bedroom across from her parents' room, listening to music on her clock radio. Soon, they were all in bed and asleep. It would be the last peaceful sleep they would have.

The following Sunday morning, Max, Clementine, and Karol woke up early and, as they regularly did, attended mass together at the Saint Alphonsus Catholic Church. The church, a large, red-brick structure with a soaring steeple, was only a half-dozen blocks west of the Beavers' home. The church sat at the crest of a low hill on the southwest side of town, not far from Saunders Park, named after the town's founder.

Sunday, October 29, 1978, developed into a beautiful fall day in Mount Pleasant. The air was cool and crisp that morning, the trees sporting leaves of brown, yellow, orange and red. It became unseasonably warm later that sunny afternoon, with a high temperature in the mid-60s. It would grow chilly later that evening, however, after the sun went down with the temperature dropping down to the upper 30s by midnight.

After lunch with her family, Karol took part in practice for the Powder Puff football game that would take place the following Wednesday evening, the first of November. Practice was held at the new athletic complex on the north side of town, not far from Beavers' Jack & Jill Market, a neighborhood grocery store Max had owned and operated by then for more than two decades. Karol drove the family van to practice. While Karol was at her Powder Puff practice, Clementine drove the family Buick to visit her elderly mother in West Point, a town of less than a thousand people southeast of Mount Pleasant. Max remained home, watching a football game on television in the basement den.

Karol returned home mid-afternoon after the Powder Puff football practice. She parked the family van in the driveway, walked through the side garage door, and came up the two steps through a door and into the kitchen. She heard the television on in the den, so she stepped downstairs to the basement. The stairs to the basement were located just inside the door leading to the garage, directly across from the kitchen. When Karol came to the bottom of the stairs she turned to the right and walked around the bar to where her father was sitting in his favorite leather chair watching a football game. She announced she was home and told him all about practice. They chatted for a while and watched a little of the game, but now that Karol had returned home with the van, Max decided after a few minutes that he would go to the store to check up on things and work on the books for an hour or two.

Clementine returned from visiting her mother in West Point shortly after Max left for the store. A little before 4:00 p.m., Karol's married older sister, Kathy, stopped by the house and persuaded Karol to attend mass with her at the Mental Health Institute chapel. Kathy had missed mass that morning and she and Karol both liked the priest at the chapel; plus, there was the added benefit that his masses were only a half-hour long. Karol drove Kathy's car to the chapel. As they drove, Kathy glanced over at her little sister, noticing what beautiful auburn hair Karol had. For a little while that late afternoon, while Karol was gone to mass and Max was pouring over bookwork at the grocery store, Clementine raked leaves in the front yard. She gathered leaves into small piles as the air began to cool. A little after 4:30 p.m., Kathy dropped Karol off at the Beavers' home then drove back to her own home across town. She would never see her mother or little sister alive again.

Max returned home around 5:30 p.m. Clementine informed Max that Karol had run out to get something to eat from the A&W restaurant on the west side of town and would be home soon. The oldest of Max and Clementine's eight children, Ron, also came over to the house at about this time. Ron and Max went downstairs and watched some of the Denver Bronchos-Seattle Sea Hawks football game on TV. Ron departed after the game ended at about the same time Karol returned home. Karol made some popcorn and then went down to the basement to watch TV with her parents for a while.

At 8:00 p.m., a new crime show that first aired in September, *Kaz*, came on the television. The program was a fictional drama featuring stories of a former convict turned defense attorney. The episode airing that evening involved a case of assault and battery by a baseball pitcher. Max watched the first fifteen minutes or so with his wife and daughter, but kept nodding off. Max had to wake up very early each morning to open the grocery store, so he went to bed early most nights. About 8:15 p.m., Max finally gave up his struggle to stay awake and announced he was heading to bed. As he stood up, Clementine asked Max to take the popcorn bowls back upstairs as they were done eating popcorn for the night. As Max climbed the stairs on the way to bed, he looked over to see Karol lying on the couch and his wife sitting in her favorite rocking chair, both watching TV.

A little bit later, around 8:45 p.m., Karol went upstairs while Clementine remained downstairs watching TV. Karol retreated to her room down the hall, turned on the light, and called her best friend, Lisa Howe. Karol was still enthralled with her ex-boyfriend, Brad Gardner. Her parents had made her break up with him because he was several years older than Karol and had graduated from high school already. Nevertheless, this night, Karol was trying to find him, to talk with him, even though her parents disapproved. She asked Lisa if she knew where Brad might be this evening because he wasn't at home, but

Lisa didn't know. Unbeknownst to Karol, Brad Gardner was with another high school girl that night.

Unable to locate Brad, Karol stayed in her room and turned on her radio to listen to music. Her radio was tuned to KGRS, a local station out of Burlington, Iowa, that played popular music. The number one song on the pop charts on October 29, 1978, was *Hot Child in the City*. Also high on the pop charts and playing that night on the radio were "Summer Nights," and other songs from the hit movie *Grease*. They were all songs about love and youth and hope. The radio played softly in her room. Karol kept the volume down so as not to wake her father who was asleep in bed across the hallway from her room.

Sometime between about 9:00 and 9:30 p.m., a man slipped into the Beavers' garage through the unlocked side door. From there, he entered the Beavers' kitchen through the unlocked door leading to the garage. He quietly shut the door behind him then paused for a moment, listening, looking. Immediately to his left he heard the noise of a television program emanating from the basement stairs. Ahead of him he heard music on a radio wafting down the hallway, coming from Karol's room. The man turned to the left and crept down the stairs to the basement. The stair treads occasionally squeaked beneath his weight, but the new carpeting muffled the sound. Clementine either didn't hear the man come down the stairs, or mistakenly believed it was Karol returning to watch TV with her.

As the man rounded the corner at the bottom of the basement stairs, he saw Clementine sitting in her rocking chair. He had likely already seen where she was sitting before even entering the home by looking through the small basement windows from the outside as he cased the house. Now, when the man had reached the basement, Clementine's back was to the stairs, and to the man. Her attention was focused on the television; she remained completely unaware of his presence.

The man stepped behind the bar and approached the back of Clementine's chair. He raised the barrel of a rifle over the top of the bar and pointed it at the back of Clementine's head, only inches away from the end of the barrel.

Then he pulled the trigger, blasting a bullet into Clementine's head.

The bullet drilled a hole in her skull, a little to the right of center and parallel with her ears. The impact of the bullet snapped Clementine's head forward killing her almost instantly. She remained sitting upright, but slumped over to the right in her chair, bleeding profusely from the back of her head.

The killer pulled back the bolt on the rifle, discharging the spent cartridge, and chambered another round. He bent over and picked up the spent cartridge, slipping it into his pocket. Then the killer stepped around the bar, past Clementine, and switched off the television. He listened for any sounds coming from upstairs, then stepped past Clementine's body, around the bar, and clambered back upstairs.

From her bedroom, Karol had heard the loud bang coming from the basement. She stepped out of her room and looked down the hallway, pausing a moment to listen.

She heard no more loud noises but hurried down the hall anyway to investigate the source of the loud noise. Karol reached the kitchen at about the same time the killer reached it coming up from the basement stairs.

Karol stopped in her tracks, startled and surprised. From the dim illumination shed by the kitchen light above the stove, Karol must have recognized the killer. The man certainly recognized her.

He quickly raised the rifle and pointed it at Karol's face. She instantly and instinctively raised her right hand in defense. The killer just as instantly fired.

The bullet passed through Karol's forearm and into her cheek, fracturing the bone just below her left eye, then passed along the side of her face before it exited just above and in front of her left ear. Karol crumpled to the kitchen floor, blood pouring from her face and arm. She moaned in pain. She likely struggled to her hands and knees and attempted to crawl away, severely but not fatally injured.

The killer stood over her, pulled back the rifle bolt discharging the spent shell casing, inserted another bullet, and chambered the new round. Then he placed the barrel of the weapon near the back of Karol's head, just above and behind her right ear, and squeezed the trigger again. The bullet pierced her skull. Karol collapsed to the floor in a pool of blood. The killer quickly pulled back the rifle bolt, discharged the spent cartridge, and chambered yet another round. Then he picked up the spent cartridges and slipped them into his pocket.

The killer paused, listened, looked. He heard no more movement inside the house. Max, in bed just down the hall in his bedroom with the door closed remained fast asleep. He didn't hear the first shot. Or the second. Or the third. Max slept on, blissfully ignorant of the horror happening in his home.

The killer stepped out of the kitchen, back out into the garage, and peered out the side garage door, into the dark street. He saw no one there. No dogs barked, though a neighbor nearby had two large dogs he kept outside who frequently barked at the slightest provocation. But not this night. This night, all was quiet and still.

The killer set the rifle against the garage wall. He stepped out of the side door to the garage and glanced up and down the street. Off in the distance he saw a car drive down a side street and away. There was no other movement on Locust Street. Lights in the neighbors' homes hadn't suddenly come on. No one was coming out of their homes to investigate the gunfire. There was no movement, no sound. No sirens blared in the distance. The neighborhood was quiet, peaceful. No one had apparently heard the gun shots. No one was alerted to the mayhem. No one knew of the monster in the Beavers' home.

The killer slipped back into the garage, shutting the door behind him, and stepped back into the kitchen. Karol still lay there on the linoleum floor in an ever-growing pool of her own blood. The killer grabbed Karol by her legs and dragged her a short distance toward the garage, then turned her around, dropped her feet. He walked around to the other side, raised her up by her armpits, and dragged her the rest of the way through the door and down two steps into the garage. He laid her down on the garage floor next to the family Buick.

Karol was still alive, still breathing, but mercifully unconscious. The killer shut the door to the kitchen. Karol lay helpless on the cold garage floor. Her face was covered with blood, still seeping from her nose, her cheek, her head, some pooling in her left ear, more beginning to pool on the garage floor. Her right forearm bled profusely where the bullet had passed through it. Karol's skin began turning pale as blood flowed from her body.

The killer bent over Karol and stripped off her sweater, her shoes, her jeans and panties, and tossed them all aside. He pulled her bloody Iowa State T-shirt up over her breasts, and yanked her bra down, exposing her left breast. He sucked on her nipple. Then he pulled down his pants, laid on top of Karol's limp and bloody body, and raped her as she lay dying on the frigid garage floor. The killer raped Karol so violently he tore her vagina. When he finished, he stood up, pulled up his pants, and left her there to die.

TWO
MY HOMETOWN MURDERS

"My hometown... was always there, at all times, unchanging. What I think... is not that we go back to our hometowns, but that someday our hometowns come back into each of our hearts."

— Jirō Taniguchi, A JOURNAL OF MY FATHER

THE FIRST TIME LAW ENFORCEMENT OFFICERS fingerprinted me, I was 16 years old. It was 1979, and the fingerprinting was part of an investigation of the murders of three women. One victim was Karol, my high school classmate. Another, her mother, Clementine, a friend of my family. The third victim was a young woman I worked with at a restaurant, beaten to death six months after Karol and Clementine were slaughtered.

The last time law enforcement officers fingerprinted me, I was 55 years old. It was 2018, and the fingerprinting was part of a routine background investigation in connection with my nomination by the President of the United States to become a United States District Court Judge.

I didn't commit those murders in my hometown of Mount Pleasant, Iowa, in the late 1970s, but I know who did. He was a classmate and coworker of mine. His name was Monte Seager.

Monte's murders sent shockwaves through the sleepy, small town of Mount Pleasant, where I grew up. This was especially so when the police revealed that my classmate had also been raped. The crimes rocked the foundation of complacency and trust that formed the character of our quiet community. For six months after the first two murders—those of my classmate and her mother—the police had no leads, identified no suspects, made no arrests. The placid and peaceful parish where people seldom locked their doors at night, where children used to play in their backyards at dusk and ride their bikes along the residential streets in the evening, became a paranoid, terrified enclave. As night fell, parents called their children in from playing in the yards, the streets became deserted, and families shut themselves inside their homes behind locked windows and doors. Women were afraid to venture anywhere alone, or even be in their homes alone.

Then, late one night six months after the shooting deaths of my classmate and her mother, a cocktail waitress was bludgeoned to death in a local restaurant. People immediately assumed there was a connection between this violent crime and the Beavers' murders. Mount Pleasant hadn't experienced crimes of violence like these before.

There was fear of a serial murderer on the loose. Based on evidence found at the scene and statements from witnesses, suspicion soon fell on Monte Seager for the murder of the waitress at the restaurant where he also worked. It wasn't long before police took a closer look at him for the two prior murders as well.

After an arrest, an escape, the suppression of evidence, two trials, and two decades, Monte Seager would ultimately be convicted of all three murders, along with other related crimes.

These murders devastated the victims' families. The murders also had a lasting and widespread impact on the community. The murder of a classmate, by a classmate, significantly impacted them. It likely contributed my late twin brother's decision to become a cop. I know it spurred my interest in the law.

As time moved inexorably on, while the authorities investigated and prosecuted Monte for the murders, I attended college and law school, became a federal prosecutor, and was ultimately appointed to a life term as a federal judge. While Monte sat by himself in a prison cell growing older behind bars serving two life terms, I started and raised a family, advanced in my career, and grew older myself. Meanwhile, the victims lived no more; their stories stopped in the late 1970s, their lives cut short and frozen in time.

As a former federal prosecutor, I investigated and prosecuted nearly a thousand criminal defendants, including multiple murderers. As a judge, I have presided over hundreds of cases, including those involving killings.

Although motive is seldom an element of these offenses, it is never far from everyone's mind. People have a fundamental desire to discover, understand, and comprehend the motive for crimes, especially murders. They want to know why someone took the life of another human being, why they killed. I am no different. In every murder case I have handled as a prosecutor and as a judge, I have always felt it necessary to get to the core of the crime, to understand what drove a person to kill.

And yet, through all these many years, Monte's murders have haunted me because I never understood why he did it. It also troubled me because some people questioned whether he really committed the murders of my classmate and her mother. Some in the community continued to question his guilt, speculating that he was wrongfully convicted. If he did commit the murders, the motive for slaughtering my classmate and her mother remained elusive. As part of a plea deal reducing his charges, Monte admitted murdering the waitress during a robbery of the restaurant. But he always maintained he was innocent of killing my classmate and her mother. He told officers who interviewed him that he didn't do it. Yet, he was twice found guilty of the murders. But because he never testified at his trials, he never explained his reasons, and the answer for why he committed the murders remained unanswered. Until now.

Decades after the murders, I decided to investigate them, not as a prosecutor or a judge, but as an author. And as a person who knew the murderer and his victims. I resolved to investigate and write about these murders in my hometown. My research would take me back in time, back to my hometown, back to friends and acquaintances, and even back to Monte himself. And he would admit to me, even though he had denied it before, that he murdered Clementine and Karol Beavers.

THREE
MOUNT PLEASANT THEN

"Every town has a psychopath or two." — MAIMED, by
Nikki Ferguson

MOUNT PLEASANT IS LOCATED IN THE ROLLING HILLS
and shallow valleys of southeast Iowa. Eastern Iowa is
laced with rivers and streams that flow like so many
converging veins to the southeast corner of the state where
they merge into each other and ultimately join up with the
mighty Mississippi River. The largest river near Mount
Pleasant, the unfortunately and unflatteringly named
Skunk River, rolls steadily along outside the southwest city
limits through the remains of a former settlement known
as Oakland Mills. The many streams flowing gently
through and near Mount Pleasant and into the Skunk
River have uncreative names such as Big Creek, Fish
Creek, and Mudd Creek; many more remain nameless.

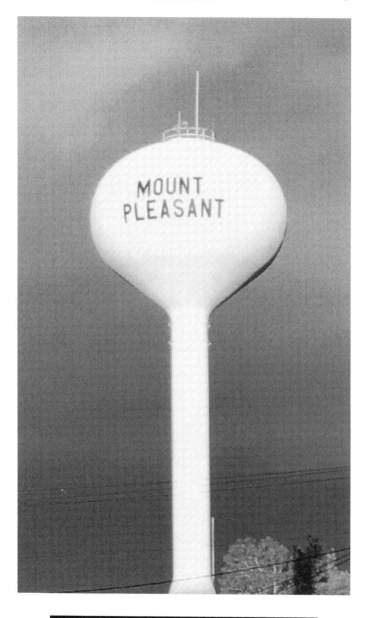

Water tower in Mount Pleasant, Iowa (photo by author)

The countryside in Southeast Iowa is dotted with small farms. The soil is rich, black, and productive. Bucolic villages and modest towns form the hubs of commerce for the surrounding farms. Mount Pleasant is one such town.

Mount Pleasant was founded in 1835 and grew by the start of the Civil War to a community of about 3,500 people, at that time about the same size as Des Moines, the state capital. For a time, Mount Pleasant became influential in state and national politics. James Harlan, a resident of Mount Pleasant, became an influential Republican United States Senator and ally of President Abraham Lincoln. Senator Harlan's daughter, Mary, would later marry Robert Todd Lincoln, President Lincoln's only surviving child. Abolitionists Frederick Douglass, Sojourner Truth, and Anna Dickinson presented lectures in Mount Pleasant. Shortly after the war, in 1869, 24-year-old Arabella "Bella" A. Mansfield of Mount Pleasant took an oath in Union Hall there, becoming the first woman in the United States to be awarded a license to practice law, a half century before women had the right to vote.

After such an auspicious beginning, though, Mount Pleasant stagnated. A century after the Civil War, Mount Pleasant had only grown to a city of about 7,000 souls. Once a teeming town on the cusp of greatness, by 1978 Mount Pleasant had slowly morphed into a quiet little farming community with no pretentions.

Nevertheless, in the 1970s, Mount Pleasant was still fairly prosperous for a small town in Iowa. Two major highways intersected the town. A railroad carrying freight and passengers also passed through the town. The town hosted a private college and several small factories. A state mental health institute and a minimum security prison shared a campus on the southeast side of town.

In the mid to late 1970s, Mount Pleasant had a moderately thriving business district occupying about an eight-square-block area surrounding the town square. The business district hosted three men's clothing stores, my father's included (named, simply enough, "Williams Clothing"). It also contained several shoe stores, including one my father owned called "The Corner Cobbler" located on the northeast side of the square. There were several women's clothing stores, drug stores, department stores, cafes, and even a few bars. One bar in particular, located on the west side of the town square, was a rather dark and seedy bar for Mount Pleasant. There was also a Coast-to-Coast hardware store on Jefferson Street, just down the block from my father's store, and up the next block from the seedy bar on the west side of the town square. My mother worked as a photographer and editor of the local newspaper, simply named "The Mount Pleasant News," located just across the street from City Hall, a block off the main square.

Businesses stretched out toward the edges of town, especially east and west of downtown on Highway 34. On the east side were some of the light industries, car dealerships, and a department store. On the west side of town were several restaurants, including fast food places like A&W and Pizza Hut, but also an upscale place called the Iris Restaurant.

In the 1970s, there were several elementary schools scattered about in Mount Pleasant including Lincoln Elementary on the south side of town. There was, however, only one middle school and one high school. The high school, located near the downtown, was built in 1932.

Mount Pleasant High School (photo by author)

High school classes typically held between 100 and 150 students. The graduating class of 1980, the class of Karol Beavers and Monte Seager was typical: it had 126 students. It would have had two more crossing the stage to receive their diplomas that May of 1980, but for what happened in October 1978.

In 1978, Mount Pleasant was a quiet little slice of the Midwest. Most people attended church, worked hard, and lived clean and fruitful, if uneventful lives. High school sports drew the townspeople like professional sporting events might draw crowds in larger cities. Friday night varsity football and basketball games were major town events. The single country club and public golf course was also popular and busy. Local businessman Max Beavers and his youngest daughter Karol placed respectfully that summer in a father-daughter golf tournament.

Nationally, the 1970s was a time of increasing social tensions. Crime was on the rise across the nation, fueled in part by drugs and in part by rebellion against a government that dragged the United States into a war in Southeast Asia. The murder rate in particular skyrocketed in the 1970s. Congress became especially concerned about so-called "Saturday Night Specials," a colloquial term used to describe compact, small-caliber, cheap handguns of poor quality that were associated with a lot of violent crime in the 1970s. Legislation to regulate the importation and manufacture of such junk guns slowly, but eventually, choked off the supply by the 1980s.

But the national crime wave largely flowed around our quiet little town. In Mount Pleasant, there was little crime in the late 1970s: a few thefts, a little marijuana smoking, an occasional drunk driver. Mount Pleasant remained a pleasant town.

Mount Pleasant had a scanty police force consisting of the Chief of Police, August "Gus" Hagers, and nine officers. Gus became a police officer simply because he needed a job after dropping out of college. He was sworn in as a peace officer in 1970 at the age of 21. After a couple years, Gus went to work at the sheriff's office for a year or so, but quit because he and the sheriff didn't get along. After managing a fast food restaurant for a year, Gus returned to the police department becoming its chief in 1977. In 1978, he was only 29 years old.

Gus Hagers (photo in Mount Pleasant Police Department)

The County Sheriff's Office was also headquartered in Mount Pleasant, where the Sheriff, Richard "Dick" Droz, had the assistance of only three or four deputies. Droz had worked in law enforcement since 1960. By 1978, Sheriff Droz was 40 years old.

Both the police department and sheriff's office shared the same building, referred to locally as the Law Enforcement Center. The building was originally a ranch-style house that had been converted for law enforcement purposes. On the main floor was a reception area, a booking room, an interview room, and cubicles for the police officers and the sheriff and his deputies. In the basement was a holding tank that could house five or six inmates overnight (typically people held for public intoxication or drunk driving or the like) and two private jail cells.

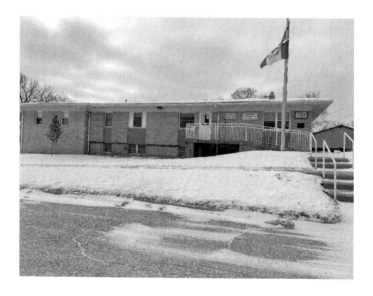

Former Mount Pleasant, Iowa Law Enforcement Center (photo by author)

Because there was little serious crime in Mount Pleasant back in the 1970s, the cells were seldom occupied. There hadn't been a homicide in Mount Pleasant since 1944. The crime problems in Mount Pleasant in 1978 were fairly tame.

At a Chamber of Commerce meeting in March 1978, merchants complained about "the problem of downtown of juveniles and young adults," hanging about in the evenings, particularly on the north side of the square. One member of the community suggested imposing a ten o'clock p.m. closing time for the parks, including the city square, instead of the current midnight closing time, to deal with the pernicious problem. But Chief Hagers and others expressed sympathy for the youths because "they have no place to go and nothing to do." Someone else suggested that launching a Junior Achievement program for youths might help. Yet another person urged local merchants to hire the young people, opining that would keep them off the streets.

At the City Council meeting in May 1978, Chief Hagers announced that "dogs and cats pose a real problem here."

Other than an aberrant and unusual death by explosion of a local car dealer a couple years before, violence was almost nonexistent in Mount Pleasant. The peaceful citizens of Mount Pleasant were very trusting. It was quite common for people to leave the keys in the ignitions of their cars, parked in the driveways of their unlocked homes. Young children played and roamed about the town at all hours of the day and night. Young women thought nothing of being alone on the streets or in their homes. There hadn't been a reported sexual assault in Mount Pleasant for as long as anyone could recall.

By happenstance, on the evening of September 15, 1978, Chief Hagers gave a public safety presentation at the Child Conservation League meeting on the topic of safety for women. He provided tips for women to remain safe. He also encouraged them to contact the police and report if they were ever raped.

A little more than a month later, Karol Beavers would be brutally raped in her home. She wouldn't be able to report it, though, as she was dead.

FOUR
THE BEAVERS

"You are the salt of the earth." THE BIBLE, Matthew 5:13

MAX AND CLEMENTINE BEAVERS WERE, AS THE colloquial phrase goes, salt of the earth folks.

Max was born the sixth of nine children and grew up in the small community of Bloomfield, Iowa, located about 60 miles southwest of Mount Pleasant. His father was a farm laborer, his mother a homemaker. Max's family moved often from farm to farm as his father struggled to find work during the Great Depression. The family ultimately settled on a farm near Mount Pleasant in the mid-1930s.

Max had a difficult childhood. His mother suffered from tuberculosis and when Max was still young she was hospitalized in a sanitarium, leaving Max's father to raise the children alone for a while. The State of Iowa initially aided the family financially while Max's mother was ill, helping his father support the family. But Max's mother was dying a slow death, and she and everyone else knew it. Max later remembered his mother holding him as a child, telling him how much she was going to miss her children.

When Max was thirteen years old, his mother died. The financial aid the state had been providing while she was ill now dried up. Unable to financially support his large family any longer while raising and caring for his children at the same time, Max's father faced a difficult dilemma. Ultimately, he decided to send all but the youngest two children away to live with others. Max himself was taken in by a farm family near New London where he stayed until he became an adult.

Max persevered through the trials and tribulations of his childhood. He grew up, graduated from high school in 1939, and took a job as a butcher in West Point, Iowa, a tiny town southeast of Mount Pleasant. There, Max met Clementine Winnike, a young woman who grew up on a farm outside of West Point. Clementine pronounced her name "Clementeen," but her friends and family called her "Clemmy" or more often, just "Clem." Clementine's parents were Clem and Agnes Winnike; they were of German heritage, like Max.

Clementine was the oldest of eight children; six girls and two boys. Clementine prided herself on always looking neat and proper. Even while doing chores on the farm she wore a dress. She didn't wear slacks until she was in her 50s; she never deigned to wear blue jeans. After Clementine graduated from high school, she took a job as a postmaster's assistant at the United States Post Office in West Point. It was while Clementine was on her lunch breaks from that job that she and Max caught each other's eye. They met in the grocery store where Max worked in West Point. Soon Max courted Clementine and they became an item.

Then on December 7, 1941, the Japanese bombed Pearl Harbor. When the United States entered World War II, Max answered the call for volunteers and signed up with the United States Army. Naturally, given his trade in civilian life, the Army assigned him to kitchen duties. After basic training, and while Max was traveling by train from his training camp in the east and his initial post on the west coast, he obtained leave and stopped off in Mount Pleasant just long enough to marry Clementine. They tied the knot on October 13, 1943.

Max went off to serve in the Pacific Theatre during the war. After his military service, he returned to Mount Pleasant. Reunited with Clementine, Max found work and they started a family. Ron, their oldest child, entered this world almost exactly nine months after Max came home from the war. Max returned to work as a butcher, at first back at the same grocery store in West Point where he had worked before the war. But soon, Max started a new job working as the butcher at a grocery store called Scotties, a small, neighborhood mom-and-pop store in Mount Pleasant.

Scotties was situated directly across the railroad tracks from the train depot, just a couple blocks north of the middle school. The manager of Scotties, a man named Joe, had been an orphan, given up for adoption as an illegitimate child, the product of an affair between a doctor and a nurse. Joe ran away from his abusive adoptive home when he was 16 and made his own way in the world, hopping from job to job. He volunteered for the Navy during World War II when he was in his mid-30s, motivated as much by a need for employment as he was by patriotism. Joe was, by then, a husband and father of two pre-teen children. After the war, Joe somehow secured employment as the manager of Scotties, though he had no prior experience running a grocery store.

Joe was my grandfather. While in high school, my father used to work in the store after school stocking shelves, bagging groceries, and cleaning up. My grandfather hired Max to run the meat market in the store.

The small Beavers family soon expanded. In the next couple years, Ron was joined by his little brothers Rick and Randy. Eventually, Max and Clementine were blessed with five more children: Kathy, Robert, Kim, Kerrie, and eventually Karol. The Beavers family moved into the apartment above the grocery store (which was later removed). They would live there for five years before moving to a small house.

Max eventually bought the store in the early 1950s and renamed it Beavers' Jack & Jill Market. My grandfather, a jack of all trades, moved on to some other job. He would eventually join my father in the clothing business.

The site of Beavers' Market (photo by author)

Running a grocery store is demanding and seemingly never-endless work. Max would arise at 4:30 every morning, six days a week, to bake fresh bread at the market and get the store ready for customers. The store was open six and half days a week, being closed only on Sunday mornings. Max continued to serve as the store's butcher, but he also managed everything else too, stocked the shelves, purchased the goods, and kept the books. The store had only two cash registers. Max employed a full time cashier and another full time employee to help out, along with some part-time help. In addition, as their children grew older, Max inevitably had them helping out at the store from an early age as free labor. From time to time, Clementine also would help out at the store, operating one of the cash registers when she wasn't otherwise busy raising the couple's children.

The store was popular and busy. At noon every day when school was in session, students from the nearby middle school would often swarm into Beavers' Market to buy ice cream, candy, and other snacks. Max and Clementine were like parents to all the school kids. They loved to see the kids as much as the kids liked to see the Beavers.

Max was of modest height, stocky, patient, and kind, with a great sense of humor. He was described by many as one of the nicest men in Mount Pleasant. When customers couldn't pay with cash, he let them charge groceries to a store account. When, on occasion, people down on their luck came into Beavers' Market and were unable to pay off their bill, Max would send them away with bags full of groceries, whether the customers could pay for them all or not.

Yet, Max was a successful businessman. Not only did he own Beavers' Market, he also eventually owned several rental properties in town. Max was also active in the community, serving on the City Council, occupying leadership positions in the local chapter of the VFW (Veterans of Foreign Wars), and as a member of the Rotary Club. Max also volunteered for the high school athletic booster club and was part of the chain gang marking yardage on the side lines when his boys played high school football. Max loved watching sports and playing sports; he especially liked to golf and go bowling. Max was also an avid card player. He knew how to play almost every card game there was. Family rumor had it that Max learned to play cards during the war and earned so much from his fellow GIs that it formed the nest egg he would eventually use to purchase the grocery store.

With his children, Max was a firm, but kind father. When the boys got out of line, once in a while he resorted to using a belt on their backsides. But, it was the humiliation of the punishment that hurt most because Max didn't really put any force behind his spanks.

Max Beavers (photo from obituary)

Clementine was a thin woman standing 5 feet, 4 inches tall. Clementine's full time job was being a mother to an increasing brood of children. By 1978, she was 58 years old with only the youngest child, Karol, still at home. Clementine was described as perpetually pleasant, unfailingly friendly, and quick to smile. She loved to laugh.

Clementine became an excellent cook and loved to bake. She attempted to accommodate the various and sometimes conflicting taste preferences of her children whenever possible, trying to make and bake their favorite foods. Clementine was very organized, as she had to be with so many children. She cooked and cleaned and maintained the house, taking care of their many children from diapers to driving. She must have washed clothes every day for many years. Yet, at the end of each day when Max came home from work, Clementine had a hot, nourishing meal on the table for him and whatever children were living at home at the time.

Although Clementine learned to play bridge for Max's sake, and belonged to a woman's bridge club, unlike Max she wasn't much of a card player outside of bridge. For many years, Clementine refrained from obtaining a driver's license. When she needed to go somewhere, she walked, hitched a ride with friends, or waited until Max could drive her where she needed to go. Eventually she took driving lessons and earned a driver's license; then she wondered why she hadn't gotten a driver's license long before.

Clementine "Clem" Beavers in the late 1970s (photo courtesy of the Beavers family)

THE HEART OF CLEMENTINE'S LIFE WERE HER children. She had eight pregnancies between 1946 and 1957; one child (Terrence) died only days after his birth. She and Max agreed that she would stay home and raise the children while he provided a living for the family. She loved the arrangement. The Beavers' children were typical rambunctious kids, playing with neighborhood children, sledding in the winter on the hill behind their home, playing on the grounds of the Lincoln Elementary School across the street in front of their home.

Lincoln playground as seen from the Beavers' front yard (photo by author)

Clementine was in charge of disciplining the children, but in practice she wasn't much of a disciplinarian. She was fairly indulgent of her children. She seldom raised her voice. Her way of dealing with her children when they misbehaved was to say, "Wait until your father gets home." That formidable phrase was usually all it took to bring the kids back into line. Clementine endeavored to cultivate a proper attitude in her children, consistent with her strong religious beliefs. She taught all her children to be respectful of and kind to all people, no matter who they were, no matter where they came from or what their background was.

Clementine was a very religious person; indeed, all the Beavers were devoted Catholics. Clementine was very active in the St. Alphonsus church on the southwest side of town. The Beavers' route from their home to their church took them right past the modest home of Harry Seager. He was the only blind man then living in Mount Pleasant. In the spring of 1978, Harry's oldest son, Monte, would return from foster care to live with him for the first time in ten years.

Clementine was the heart of the family, the one everyone sought in times of crisis. She was the glue that held the family together. And Clementine was a very caring and compassionate person. She especially doted on her children and grandchildren. They were the source of her greatest happiness. In 1978, Clementine was blessed with four more grandchildren, adding to the two other grandchildren born in the preceding years. She adored her grandchildren and they adored her.

Every other Sunday, Clementine would return home to her family farm a short distance away in the little village of West Point, Iowa, population 911, taking one or more of the kids in tow. The children loved playing on the farm with their cousins. In 1978, Clementine's 86-year-old mother was still living on her own in West Point. Even after the kids were pretty much grown and gone, Clementine still returned at least every other Sunday to look after and visit her mother.

After most of the children had grown up, Clementine returned to work for the first time since she married Max. She began working part time at Beavers' Market. She found great joy in the work. She loved interacting with people and particularly enjoyed the children who came into the store.

Clementine Beavers (photo from Mount Pleasant News)

In 1961, Max had a new home built at 509 South Locust Street, right across the street from Lincoln Elementary School, on the northwest side of McMillan Park. The house was only a half-dozen blocks south of the high school. The Beavers' children often walked home for lunch, it was so close. The Beavers' home, clad in tan brick, was a ranch-style structure with four bedrooms on the main floor and a two-stall garage. When the kids were young, all four boys had to share a single bedroom; the girls occupied the others. In the mid-1960s, a few years after Karol was born, the Beavers finished the basement of the home. Down there, they added a fifth bedroom where two of the boys slept. They also had a built-in bar and a den or family room area where the family's one television reigned.

Beavers' residence (photo by author)

Beavers' residence (photo by author)

My family lived in another ranch house, about a mile away, on the other side of McMillan Park. Mount Pleasant was the kind of small town where most people knew each other. My family knew the Beavers, and they knew us. My father was a small business owner like Max, operating his clothing and shoe stores. Max and my father both belonged to the Rotary Club and the Country Club. Although our two families didn't socialize as such, we knew each other well and on a first-name basis. We knew each other well enough that when I attended middle school, if Beavers' Market was swamped over the lunch hour by students, I would often step behind the counter and run one of the cash registers just to help the Beavers deal with the crush of students, though I was never employed there.

On October 13, 1978, the family celebrated Max and Clementine's 35th wedding anniversary at their daughter Kathy's home.

Clementine and Max Beavers (photo, circa early 1970s, courtesy of the Beavers family)

Max and Clementine's youngest and ninth child, a daughter, arrived late in their relationship, when Clementine was 42 years old. Karol was born on the evening of April 22, 1962. She was a year younger than my older brother, Dave, and year older than my twin brother and me. By the time Karol was born, all her brothers and sisters were either out of the house or were in high school. As the baby of the family, she was pampered and spoiled by all.

Karol Beavers (photo from Mount Pleasant News*)*

KAROL RECEIVED A DIPLOMA FROM CANDY LANE Preschool, a school my brothers and I also attended, located in a small house near the Mount Pleasant High School. She attended Kindergarten and grade school at Lincoln School, known by kids as "Stink'n Lincoln," literally across the street from her house. She received her first communion in 1970, and was confirmed in her faith in 1975. She attended middle school just down the block from her family's grocery store, and then in 1976 started high school as a freshman.

In 1978, Karol was 16 years old and a high school junior. She was the only child living at home by then. Her siblings were much older than Karol and several had moved away already, so it was very much as if Karol was an only child in many ways.

Karol was a cute, freckled-faced, spunky, and tiny girl. She stood 5 feet, one and a half inches tall and weighed about 100 pounds. Karol had long auburn hair, bright blue eyes, and an infectious smile. She was very bubbly and laughed often. "Boisterous," was the adjective one teacher used to describe her.

Neither spoiled nor stuck up, Karol was friendly with everyone. One classmate described her as a "great girl" who would "do anything for anybody." She had a good reputation among students. She floated in social circles between her class and the class ahead of hers, my older brother's class. She lived in a neighborhood near a number of students in the class ahead of hers, leading her to become close to many of them. My older brother, Dave, was good friends with Karol. He remembers that just before his senior year of high school, in the summer of 1978, he played tackle football with Karol and other neighborhood kids in the backyard of the Beavers' home.

Karol was also a good babysitter. She babysat for other families, but more often than not she babysat for her siblings' kids. By 1978, Max and Clementine had three grandchildren, the most recent one being born in January 1978. Karol adored her nephews and nieces.

Karol was very popular and well-liked by all the students. She was one of those girls that no one, not even other girls, seemed to have bad things to say about. Karol had many friends, but her best friends were classmates Lisa Howe and Cathy Whaley. They had been friends for years and spent a lot of time together. Karol shared locker 101 with Lisa. Their locker wasn't far from mine in the high school hallway, on the first floor, just a short distance from the principal's office.

I wasn't personally as close with Karol as my brother Dave was. Karol was more of an acquaintance to me, honestly, than a friend. But I knew her as one of the sincerely nice girls in school. What I remember most about Karol was her laugh. She seemed to laugh a lot. I remember often seeing her standing outside her locker between classes, chatting and laughing with other students. She seemed very happy. Indeed, I don't ever remember seeing her when she wasn't either laughing or smiling.

Karol was a good student and earned good grades—always A's and B's. As a freshman in high school, she was ranked first in a class of 168. She already knew at age 16 that she wanted to study architecture at Iowa State University. Her dream was to design homes.

Karol also was quite active in many extracurricular activities; she played the flute in the school orchestra and piccolo in marching band, served on the student council, was a cheerleader for both wrestling and football, participated in 4H, and ran on the track team. Incredibly, Karol ran hurdles, despite her diminutive size, and ran them well. She made up in energy and spring in her legs what she lack in height.

Karol was a leader and often volunteered to head up school projects. In October 1978, for example, Karol volunteered to head up building the junior class float for the homecoming parade. For a couple weeks while it was under construction, the chicken-wire and tissue work-in-progress was parked in the Beavers' attached garage until it was time for the parade, the same garage where Karol would later die.

Karol and many of her fellow classmates worked on the float, stuffing tissues into the chicken-wire and painting it. It was towed out of the garage on Thursday, October 5, to be a part of the homecoming parade that day. The Mount Pleasant High School Homecoming in 1978 was on Friday, October 6. Karol was there at the football game with her classmates, cheering on the Mount Pleasant Panthers varsity team to a win over the Washington Demons. My older brother and Karol's friend, Dave, was captain of the winning football team.

Karol started dating in high school, going "steady" from time to time with one boy or another. Karol had most recently been dating a 20-year old, Brad Gardner. He had graduated from a high school in Davenport in 1976 and had briefly attended a community college in Burlington where he reportedly never cracked open a book. After he dropped out of college, he came to live with his uncle in Mount Pleasant. He was working at a grain elevator in 1978. Karol's parents didn't approve of Karol dating him because Brad was so much older than Karol. Under pressure from her parents, Karol broke up with Brad late that summer of 1978, but secretly she still pined for him. Unfortunately for her, by October 1978, Brad had moved on to another girl.

In the fall of 1978, Karol had also been seeing a lot of Lance Poock, a classmate of hers who lived just two doors down from Karol's home. They had known each other since grade school. Lance and Karol and other friends would play cards in Karol's basement. Lance and Karol were in band together. Karol's relationship with Lance was really more one of a close friendship, however, than anything romantic.

And Karol was a "good girl." She was a little ornery and would pull pranks like TP'ing houses and other such juvenile shenanigans. She wasn't known to be sexually active and she didn't do drugs. Like most bored high school students her age living in Mount Pleasant where the Chief of Police had noted there was so little to do, she would occasionally drink alcohol at parties. We all did, back then. But that was as wild as Karol ever got.

The reality was that the Beavers family homelife of Max, Clementine, and Karol, was sedate and routine. They usually ate dinners together as a family. Most evenings Karol would finish her homework, attend school activities, or watch television. Most nights, Max would go to bed early, usually by 8:00 or 9:00 p.m., because he had to open the grocery store so early each morning. Clementine usually stayed up later watching TV, but would invariably go to bed by 10:00 p.m.; she didn't like to watch the nightly news because she found it depressing. Although most people in Mount Pleasant didn't lock their doors at night, it was part of Clementine's routine each night before she went to bed to lock the front door and the door leading to the garage from the kitchen. She always left the light on over the stove in the kitchen for when Max got up early in the morning.

FIVE
MAX'S DISASTROUS DISCOVERY

"No doubt every crime scene is a disaster for someone, it's only a question of scope."
— John Houde, Crime Lab: A Guide for Nonscientists

A little after 1:00 a.m., on October 30, 1978, Max awoke in the night needing to use the bathroom. Surprised at not finding his Clem in bed next to him as usual, Max called out: "Mom?" Hearing no reply, Max climbed out of bed, slipped on a pair of pants, and stepped out into the hallway to find out why his wife had not come to bed. The light was on in Karol's room and her radio was still playing softly, but Max didn't see his daughter in there. Max didn't think much of that at first because it wasn't uncommon for Karol to leave the lights on and her radio playing in her room, even when she was downstairs watching television.

Max decided to venture downstairs to find out why his wife and daughter were staying up so late watching TV. When he reached the kitchen from the glow of the dim light over the kitchen stove Max observed a significant amount of blood on the linoleum floor. A smeared trail of blood led to the garage. Max speculated at first that Clementine or Karol must have cut themselves pretty badly in the kitchen. Max followed the trail to the garage, thinking perhaps they took one of the cars to the hospital. When he opened the garage door he suddenly beheld his young daughter Karol lying nearly naked on the garage floor in a pool of blood. Max quickly stepped down the two steps into the garage and knelt down beside his daughter. He reached out and touched her naked, bloody torso. She was cold. Very cold. And lifeless.

Max rose up and stumbled back in to the kitchen. He tried to call the police using the phone on the kitchen counter. He smeared blood, his daughter's blood, on the phone, and tracked some across the kitchen floor.

Max was so upset and in shock he misdialed the telephone, calling a stranger instead of the police (this was back when we didn't have the 911 emergency call system and one had to dial the telephone number for the police department on a rotary phone).

Jerry Beachy, whose phone number was one digit different from the Mount Pleasant Police Department's number, answered his phone at about 1:30 a.m. When he said hello, Max's words came out in a jumbled and confusing rush, but Beachy still managed to make out that the man on the phone needed help.

"Is this the police?" Max asked.

"No," Jerry Beachy replied.

Max either didn't hear Beachy's response, or it just didn't register in Max's muddled mind because Max continued in the same vein, attempting to provide the essential information the police would need to render aid.

"This is Max Beavers and I think, I think there has, there has been a murder. My address is 509 South Locust."

Then Beachy's response seemed to get processed through the fog and confusion of Max's brain.

"Is this the police?" Max asked again.

"No, no, this isn't the police," Beechy responded, "but I will call for you." Beachy offered.

"Yeah, okay," Max replied. "Will you please hurry."

Then Max hung up the receiver. Beachy immediately called the police.

Max then turned and climbed down the stairs to the basement, looking for Clementine. He found his wife slumped over in her chair in front of the TV. He saw blood on her right shoulder and some more blood trickling out of her nose. Growing increasingly hysterical and distraught, Max quickly climbed back upstairs. When he reached the kitchen again he picked up the phone and called his two sons, first Ron then Robert. Sobbing, he begged them to come over quick. When he called Ron, Max was so shook up that he wasn't coherent about what happened. All Ron could gather from his father was that something bad had happened and to come quick. When

Max finished the hurried call with Robert, he didn't quite manage to place the receiver back on the phone's cradle. The boys rushed over to their parents' home.

Sergeant Terry Duncan was the first officer to arrive on the scene. He had been on break at the police department when the call came in from dispatch around 1:40 a.m. The only information Sergeant Duncan received from the dispatcher was a report of a possible killing at the Beavers' residence. It took Sergeant Duncan less than five minutes to run out of the Law Enforcement Center, jump in his squad car, and drive the half-dozen or so blocks to the Beavers' residence.

Arriving at the scene, Sergeant Duncan jumped out of his squad car, grabbing a flashlight. As he approached the residence, a little before 2:00 a.m., he noticed the side door to the garage was ajar. There was only a dim light on in the house. A nearby streetlight shed some light over the front yard and a little way into the open garage door. Sergeant Duncan flipped on his flashlight and panned the surroundings with its beam, but didn't see anything suspicious at first. He called for backup and waited for the only other officer on duty to arrive.

As he waited for the other officer, Sergeant Duncan suddenly heard some movement inside the garage and the sound of a man's voice. The man was yelling and hollering something, but Sergeant Duncan couldn't make out what he was saying. Approaching closer and glancing through the open side door to the garage, Sergeant Duncan could see from the beam of his flashlight a body of a mostly naked woman lying on the garage floor.

Sergeant Duncan drew his service weapon, a powerful .357 magnum revolver, and demanded whoever was in the garage to come out, hands up. When no one immediately came out, he shouted out the command a second time.

A second or two later, Max wandered, stumbling out the door to the house and into the garage, disoriented, in shock. It was so dark in the garage, Sergeant Duncan couldn't make out who it was. He did notice, though, that the man was only partially dressed, wearing pants, with an unbuckled belt, and a white T-shirt, but no socks or shoes. The man's hair was uncombed and askew.

Sergeant Duncan ordered the man to stop, but Max didn't. Max stepped over the body of his daughter and kept walking toward the officer. Max's arms were down by his sides, but his hands were moving quickly, spastically, without purpose or direction.

Sergeant Duncan yelled another command for the man to raise his hands. Max just kept coming.

Sergeant Duncan yelled again, ordering the man to stop. But Max kept walking toward the officer, mumbling incoherently, his hands moving everywhere except up where Sergeant Duncan had ordered him to place them. As the man drew closer, Sergeant Duncan could now see blood on the man's clothes. Sergeant Duncan would later tell me that, as Max ignored his orders and kept walking closer and closer to him, Sergeant Duncan's finger drew tighter and tighter on the trigger of his revolver, leveled at Max's chest. Sergeant Duncan was about to fire.

Just as Max emerged from the side garage door, the street light on the corner shed just enough light on Max's face that Sergeant Duncan recognized him. Sergeant Duncan had been in Beavers' Market a few times over the years and had seen Max there before. He knew Max to be the store owner. At this instant, Sergeant Duncan rapidly concluded he was the homeowner and likely victim, not suspect. Sergeant Duncan quickly released his pressure on the trigger. Had he not recognized Max, it is likely that Sergeant Duncan would have shot him.

"Something has happened to my family," Max finally managed to say in his dazed state as he drew close to Sergeant Duncan. Max mumbled something more, but indistinct, about his daughter in the garage and his wife in the basement. Sergeant Duncan could tell that Max was in a hysterical state, his hands continuing to constantly move about aimlessly and rapidly.

About then, the backup officer arrived, as did Max's son, Ron. Another son, Robert, arrived a minute later. It was cold outside and Max was shaking both from the cold and from shock. Together, Max's sons took care of him at the scene. But Sergeant Duncan was concerned about Max's condition and instructed them to take Max to the hospital to be treated for shock. Max was released from the hospital to his family's care later that day. Only later did officers think of testing Max's hands for gunshot residue that might have remained on his hands had he been the killer.

Meanwhile, Sergeant Duncan knew he had to continue to investigate the crime scene. He felt certain, indeed convinced, that the killer was still inside. He didn't know if anyone else was alive in the house. He didn't know if the girl on the garage floor was still alive. For all he knew, Max's wife was hiding from the killer in the basement. He had to go in, and he had to go in now. There wasn't time to wait for more off-duty officers to arrive.

Sergeant Duncan's backup officer who had just arrived, the only other officer on duty, was a rookie. Sergeant Duncan would need that young officer to secure the outside of the house in case the killer tried to escape out of the house through a back door or window as Sergeant Duncan entered the house through the garage. Sergeant Duncan realized that he would have to go into the house alone. So, Sergeant Duncan ordered the rookie backup officer to secure the outside of the house as best he could, by himself, while Sergeant Duncan entered the house, by himself.

Still with his gun drawn, Sergeant Duncan slowly approached the side garage door. Holding his flashlight in one hand and his revolver in the other, Sergeant Duncan stepped into the garage. He scanned the inside of the garage, the beam from the light illuminating the dark corners. Seeing no one present, he focused the beam before him.

Sergeant Duncan observed Karol's body on the cold garage floor, lying between a car and the door leading into the house. Karol was laying on her back with her head toward the front of the house. Karol's head was turned to her right side, her once-beautiful auburn hair a bloody, tangled mess. Her right arm was up over her head, her left arm out to the side. Both hands were bloody. Karol's right leg was splayed out almost straight from her hips, but her left leg was bent at the knee and spread out. She was clad only in socks from the waist down.

Sergeant Duncan approached and knelt down next to Karol. With his gun still at the ready in one hand, he set down his flashlight and checked for a pulse on Karol's neck with his free hand. Her body was cold and he felt no pulse.

Sergeant Duncan rose up and advanced into the house, his revolver drawn and his flashlight splitting the darkness with its beam. When he stepped through the garage door into the kitchen, he immediately saw the smeared trail of blood, about two feet wide and fifteen feet long, leading to the garage from the kitchen. He proceeded, gun still drawn, to step around the blood trail and through the kitchen to check all the other rooms on the main floor of the house. He found all the rooms upstairs empty. He noticed the bed in Karol's room was made, and the lights and radio were on. There was only static playing on the radio now the station having gone off the air more than an hour ago. The sheets on the bed in the room across the hall, the one Max and Clementine shared, were ruffled, showing someone had recently been sleeping in them. But there was no one, alive or dead, on the main floor.

Finding no one upstairs, Sergeant Duncan then proceeded carefully back through the kitchen and down the stairs into the basement. As he slowly descended the stairs, gun at the ready, he was overwhelmed with fear. He was operating under the assumption that the killer was still in the house, and he was now convinced the killer must be in the basement because he wasn't upstairs. There would be no way out for the killer except through Sergeant Duncan. As he descended the stairs into the basement, Sergeant Duncan resolved to himself that the killer would not make it past him.

As Sergeant Duncan reached the bottom of the stairs, he could hear the sound of something dripping. He thought to himself it must be coming from a sink or shower somewhere in the basement. As he rounded the corner at the bottom of the stairs he saw Clementine slumped over in her chair. He found the source of the noise. Blood was dripping from Clementine onto a puddle forming on the floor beneath her.

Sergeant Duncan approached Clementine's chair. With one hand, he felt for a pulse. He noticed her body was still warm to the touch, but he sensed no pulse. Yet, he noted that blood was still actively dripping from her nose. Thinking that this might be a sign that she was still alive, Sergeant Duncan immediately called for an ambulance, then cleared the rest of the basement and confirmed there was no one else present.

Other law enforcement officers rapidly descended upon the crime scene, including sheriff's deputies and off-duty police officers. The Chief of Police, Gus Hagers, lived only a couple blocks away from the Beavers' residence; across the school yard and on the opposite side of Lincoln Elementary. After dispatch awoke him from his slumber, Chief Hagers rapidly dressed and rushed over to the Beavers' home. He didn't see anyone suspicious on the way. Once he arrived at the Beavers' house, the Chief took command and secured the premises, not allowing anyone else to enter the crime scene. With the aid of other officers, he roped off the scene by literally tying a rope from tree to tree around the house.

The Chief quickly called in the Iowa Bureau of Criminal Investigation (now known at the Iowa Division of Criminal Investigation), the state equivalent of the Federal Bureau of Investigation. The BCI had highly trained special agents who had the expertise to investigate major cases, such as murders. It was common for small town police departments that lacked their own homicide investigation units to call upon state investigators in situations like this. The nearest BCI agent, Ron Mower, lived in Burlington and arrived about an hour later. But the crime scene investigators, the real experts, were located in Des Moines, a three hour drive away. The crime scene investigators ultimately arrived in the early morning hours, as dawn was breaking over Mount Pleasant, and took over the crime scene investigation.

Outside the Beavers' residence, the day after the murders (photo by Mount Pleasant News, *taken by my mother)*

The Chief of Police also called in my mother. Back in those days, photography was a learned and technical skill. In the 1970s, no one had cellular phones with built-in cameras like today. The average beat cop then didn't have a regular camera either, let alone the skills to use one under various and challenging lighting conditions. A small police department, like the one in Mount Pleasant, didn't have trained crime scene investigators.

Instead, it was customary back in that day for small, local police departments to call upon one of the local newspaper's staffers to serve as crime scene photographers. I recall my mother serving in that capacity many times at both crime scenes and automobile accidents and the like. It was a highly unpleasant, collateral duty of being a photographer for the local paper in a small town. On this night, the cops reached my mother after first unsuccessfully trying to call the other male news photographers.

Thus it was then in the early morning hours my

mother drove to the Beavers' home, just on the other side of McMillan Park from our house, to take photographs at the murder scene. Fortunately for my mother, Chief Hagers limited her photos to only the outside of the house, deeming it best to await BCI crime scene photographers to arrive from Des Moines to take photos of the bodies. Still, my mother would never speak about what she saw or the horror of that night.

I remember being woken up around 4:00 a.m. by the sound of my mother's sobbing coming from the living room. I came out of my bedroom to investigate and found my mother and father, together with their good friends, the newspaper's editor and his wife, sitting in the living room as my mother recounted what happened between sobs. They all had drinks in their hands.

At the scene of the Beavers' murder, the forensic investigators found Clementine still sitting upright in her chair, dead from a gunshot wound to the back of the head. Her head was slumped forward and to the right; her hands lay gently in her lap. There was vomitus matter and blood down the front of her sweater and onto her right leg. Blood from the back of her head had run down her back, soaking the chair and the carpet beneath her. Blood had also seeped from her nose and onto her shirt.

The forensic investigators found Karol lying on her back in the garage, naked from the waist down, except for her blue socks. Her body was bloody and dirty from the garage floor, fall leaves and other debris sticking to her body. Karol was wearing a yellow Iowa State T-shirt. The killer had pulled off her sweater and tossed it aside. Her T-shirt was pulled up over her breasts and covered in blood. Her bra was pulled down to reveal her left breast. The forensic investigators observed Karol's shoes, jeans, and panties laying nearby where the killer had tossed them when he stripped her. They collected the clothing and would later examine every inch of the clothing under microscopes.

The Beavers' family Buick was parked in the garage, next to Karol's body. The keys were still in the ignition (as was common back then). The forensic investigators searched the car, but found nothing of evidentiary value. They turned on the car's ignition to check the mileage and note the radio's volume and the station it was tuned to. The investigators noticed bloody footprints on the far side of the car and took photos of the pattern the soles of the shoes left in blood on the garage floor.

Investigators inspected the whole house, noting which beds were made and which were unmade, what lights were on and which were off, how the furniture was arranged, and where things were located. They drew a rudimentary sketch of the scene, which they later had converted to a scale schematic drawing. The latter drawing was of a type very like those, perhaps, that Karol would have drawn one day for other purposes had her dream to become an architect come true.

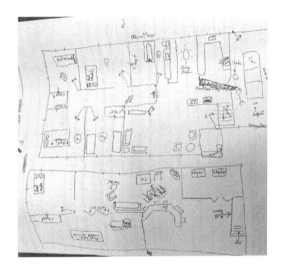

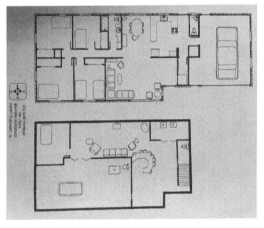

Floor plans of Beavers' residence (photos by author from police file)

The investigating officers observed there was no sign any of the rooms had been ransacked. No furniture was knocked over, no drawers were left open, nothing was obviously missing. In the first bedroom on the right down the hall, just past the dining room, there was even $290 cash sitting undisturbed in plain view on the dresser. Investigators did find a woman's purse upside down near the kitchen counter, some of the contents having spilled onto the floor. But nothing seemed to be missing from it; rather, it appeared that the purse had been knocked over by someone, perhaps by Max when he used the nearby phone to call for help.

In a hall closet, officers found a shotgun and two rifles, one of which was .22 caliber. The firearms belonged to the Beavers' grown boys who had long since moved out of the home. There was no ammunition present with the guns and later ballistics tests soon ruled out any of these firearms as the murder weapon.

In the kitchen, investigators observed the large pool of blood smeared in a long trail from the kitchen floor out through the garage door. The blood had been there long enough for some of it to have coagulated before Karol's body was dragged through it and into the garage. The amount of time it would take for blood to coagulate under those conditions was later determined to take anywhere from about 3 to 10 to 25 minutes (the estimates varied, depending on who you asked). Based on this, the forensic scientists estimated that Karol may have laid on the kitchen floor for as long as twenty-five minutes before the killer dragged her into the garage and raped her. There were also some bloody footprints in a trail as Max passed through his daughter's blood to reach the phone he used to call for help. Likewise, there was also some blood on the phone itself that came from Max's hands after touching his daughter's body to check for a sign of life.

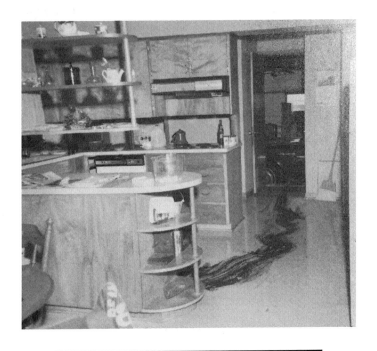

Blood trail from kitchen to garage (photo contained in police file)

A pathologist later determined that the final gunshot to the back of Karol's head would have incapacitated her, but would not have immediately killed her. Unlike the gunshot to Clementine's head, the bullet in Karol's head didn't pass through any critical areas of her brain. Rather, the pathologist estimated that Karol would have lived for anywhere from a half-hour to several hours after being shot. The first shot through her arm and into her face would have been extremely painful and her wounds would have bled profusely, the pathologist later testified. The gunshot to her face fractured her cheekbone, so the impact could easily have knocked her down. The pathologist couldn't say whether Karol would have been able to move at all after the second gunshot into the back of her head. Nor could he speculate as to whether she would have been conscious or in pain, after the second gunshot to her head. But active bleeding from the wound to her vagina when the killer raped her showed that she was still alive when the killer sexually assaulted her.

As would be expected, officers dusted for fingerprints everywhere. The investigators found some latent fingerprints—fingerprints left by a person on the surface of an object—on the fender of the Buick in the garage, next to where Karol was raped and died. Forensic scientists would compare those prints against many suspects in the ensuing years, as well as all family members and police officers who had been at the scene, but the authorities were never able to match the latent prints to anyone. Other than that one set of fingerprints, officers found no other latent prints that didn't belong to one of the Beavers family members. One pubic hair, not belonging to Karol, was also found on her jeans, along with a blond hair that also didn't belong to Karol.

Officers learned from family members that Clementine had given Karol a necklace and locket on Karol's birthday about six months before, on April 22. The heart-shaped locket had a flower design etched on it, hanging from an 18 to 20-inch gold chain. Family members told the police that Karol always wore the necklace and never took it off. Indeed, it is clearly visible in a photo taken of Karol when she gave her speech about babysitting only a few weeks before she was murdered. Yet, the police didn't find the necklace on Karol's body. Nor did investigators find it on the garage floor, in her room, or anywhere else in the house. It was missing and presumed taken at the time of her murder by the killer. It would never be found.

Officers eventually called a local funeral home whose undertakers came with a hearse. They transferred Karol's body onto a gurney and covered it with a sheet and placed her in the hearse first, pushing her body up toward the front as far as it would go so there would be room for her mother. They then recovered Clementine's body from the basement. The undertakers took both victims' bodies at first to the funeral home. Later that day, at the direction of the authorities, the victims' bodies were transported to the University of Iowa Hospital in Iowa City where a pathologist performed autopsies.

At the autopsy, the pathologist swabbed around Karol's exposed breast for any latent fluids and recovered saliva from her nipple. The pathologist also recovered semen from Karol's vagina. Back in 1978, there was no technology available that could compare the DNA in recovered semen, blood, or other bodily fluids to any suspect's DNA. The most that forensic scientists could tell back then was, sometimes, the blood type of the perpetrator. Some people are blood type secretors, meaning that their blood cells are also present in other body fluids, like saliva and semen. In this case, it turned out, the rapist was a blood Type O secretor. About 40-45% of people have Type O blood. About sixty-one percent of people with Type O blood are secretors. So, about 35% of the population are Type O secretors. The forensic testing narrowed the field of possible suspects, but not by much.

At the autopsy, attending agents observed what appeared to them to be a belt buckle-type impression in blood on Karol's shirt, possibly made by a large western style-type buckle with a word or words on the buckle. Later magnified examination of the mark seemed to suggest the impression of a letter "N" in the blood on the T-shirt. Agents also considered that it was possible, however, that the mark was made by the strap used to secure Karol to the gurney when the morticians removed her body from the house. Nevertheless, officers would include a search for large belt buckles in their investigation for years afterwards.

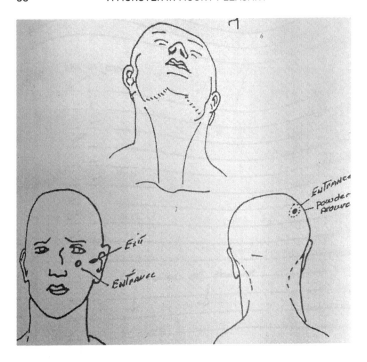

Location of wounds to Karol Beavers (photo by author of diagram contained in police file)

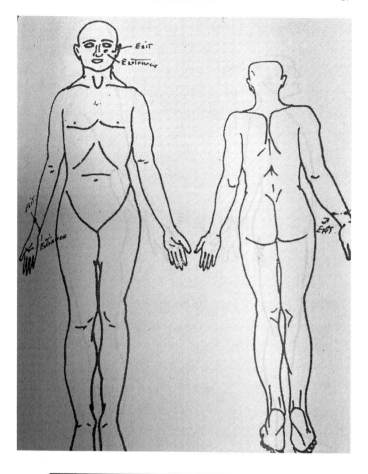

Location of wounds to Karol Beavers (photo by author of diagram contained in police file)

Based on the results of the autopsies and other evidence from the scene, the medical examiner determined that both Clementine and Karol died as a result of the gunshots to the backs of their heads. The bullet recovered from Clementine's head was still relatively intact; the one recovered from Karol's head was very mangled. The medical examiner noted stripling at all of the entrance sites, meaning all three bullets were discharged in near point-blank range. The medical examiner didn't find in her body the bullet that passed through Karol's arm and hit her cheek. Rather, the medical examiner concluded that the bullet exited her face, from her cheek, near her left ear. Despite later thoroughly searching the residence, including tearing out the carpet and using metal detectors, officers were never able to find that first spent bullet at the crime scene.

Also conspicuous by their absence were any shell casings. This led the police to believe the murderer had used a handgun, in particular a revolver. Indeed, the authorities suspected the killer used a so-called Saturday Night Special revolver because they were so prevalent then and so often used in crime nationwide.

Investigators suspected the killer used a revolver because a revolver doesn't eject shell casings. After a round is discharged, the cylinder rotates to the next chamber, while the shell casing from the discharged round remains in the chamber. A pistol, in contrast, ejects the shell casing as the explosion of the discharge of a bullet causes the slide on the weapon to rack backwards, and a spring pushes the next bullet upward, feeding it into the opening to chamber the next round. Although it was possible the killer could have used a pistol and later picked up the shell casings, that seemed improbable and would suggest an extremely careful killer. So, the evidence pointed to the use of a revolver instead of a pistol.

The officers also presumed that the murder weapon was a handgun and not a rifle. A rifle is an unwieldy and clumsy weapon to use in close quarters, such as in a house. It seemed obvious that the murderer would have used an easily-manipulated handgun instead. Common sense would also suggest that the murderer would use a handgun because it would be more easily concealable. Also, a handgun typically could be discharged much more rapidly than a rifle. Most rifles back then, outside of those used by the military and law enforcement agencies, were single-shot rifles operated by bolt action. Few rifles then were semi-automatic, so chambering a new round after each shot would be time-consuming. In contrast, the killer could fire a revolver or pistol as rapidly as he could pull the trigger. In short, with its large size and reloading procedure, a rifle would be a cumbersome murder weapon indeed, and therefore an unlikely one. Also, a rifle would have discharged shell casings with each shot, and no shell casings were found at the scene. In short, it seemed obvious to the police that the killer used a handgun to kill the Beavers, and probably a Saturday Night Special. So, that's what they began to look for.

What the officers didn't know at the time is that the killer had indeed used a bolt-action rifle. And had, indeed, picked up the shell casings. In fact, he might also have found and picked up the spent slug that passed through Karol's arm and through her cheek. It would never be found.

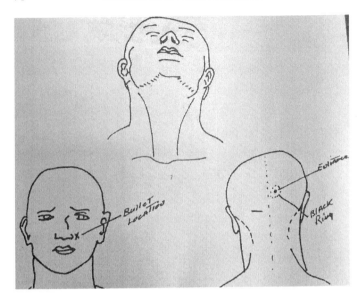

Location of wound to Clementine Beavers (photo by author of diagrams contained in police file)

A ballistics expert determined that the murder weapon was a .22 caliber firearm. The expert was also able to identify the type of ammunition used. Specifically, the killer used Cascade Cartridge, Inc. ("CCI") brand ammunition, a common brand available at most discount stores. This brand of ammunition came in both "longs" and "shorts," meaning longer and shorter cartridges. A long cartridge would hold a little more gunpowder than a short one, resulting in a slightly higher velocity upon discharge. A later analysis conducted by a ballistics expert on November 4, 1978, concluded that there was a 60% chance the murder weapon was a Rohn revolver, a 20% chance it was a Mossberg rifle, and a remaining 20%

chance that it was any one of three or four other makes and models of handguns.

A .22 caliber bullet is small—one of the smallest caliber of bullets made. It's about two or three times the size of a BB used in kids' BB guns. What most people don't know, however, is that a small caliber bullet can be extremely deadly despite its small size. The bullet cartridge, because it is small like the bullet at the end of the cartridge, contains relatively little gun powder. When a firearm hammer strikes the firing pin in the center of the cartridge, it ignites the gunpowder and the explosion sends the .22 caliber bullet down and out the gun barrel. But there is so little gun powder in a .22 caliber cartridge— even a long cartridge—that the bullet doesn't leave the barrel of the weapon with much velocity relative to larger caliber bullets. Thus, when it penetrates the human body, a .22 caliber bullet loses what little velocity it started with very rapidly. It seldom has enough velocity to exit the body. In other words, a .22 caliber bullet infrequently results in a through and through wound, meaning wounds caused by the bullet entering and exiting the body. Rather, there is often an entrance wound only and the bullet remains in the body.

With Clementine, the bullet pierced her skull in the back of her head and then ricocheted around through her soft brain tissue, bouncing off the inside of her skull, until the bullet's velocity ultimately dissipated, the bullet lodging just above her upper lip and beneath her nose. With Karol, the bullet entered the back of her head but by chance immediately lodged in the bone structure in the front of her face instead of ricocheting around. The bullet in Karol's head, as a result, was much more mangled than the one recovered from Clementine.

The medical examiner couldn't establish a time of death for either victim with any certainty. The best he could estimate was that the victims died sometime within a few hours of when they each last ate, based on the contents of their stomachs. From what officers learned, Clementine and Karol ate around 6:00 p.m. the night before, meaning that they were likely killed sometime between then and about 10:00 p.m. A later toxicology report showed no drugs or alcohol in either Karol's or Clementine's systems.

As it slowly became light outside on the morning of October 30, 1978, law enforcement officers spread out and searched the neighborhood for anyone or any clue. Officers traveled house to house, knocking on doors, asking neighbors if they had heard anything, seen anything, knew anything. Unfortunately, not a single neighbor had anything to offer. No one heard the gun shots. No one saw anyone suspicious. No one knew anything helpful to the investigation.

A couple houses away from the Beavers lived another classmate of mine, Jim Arnold. When he was a young boy, Jim's father built a tree house in the branches of a Maple tree in their backyard for Jim and his little brother. Jim watched that morning as he prepared for school as police officers, with weapons drawn, climbed the ladder and searched his tree house. They found nothing.

Later that Monday morning, the police finally gave a

statement to the press. The lead investigator candidly confided to the press, "We have no suspects and no one in custody." In fact, days, weeks, and months would go by, and still investigators had no suspects and made no arrests. For sixth months following the Beavers' murders, law enforcement officials lacked any solid leads, though they worked diligently and tirelessly trying to solve the murders.

SIX
THE SEAGERS

"The common argument that crime is caused by poverty is a kind of slander on the poor." – H. L. Mencken

MONTE SEAGER WAS THE PRODUCT OF A BROKEN home, and of foster and group homes. The Seager family was poor. And unlucky.

Monte's father, Harry, was born in 1938 and grew up in Mount Pleasant. He was raised in a middle-class family. He had three older brothers, all of whom graduated from high school, worked in the construction field, and raised families in the community. Harry was in my aunt's grade in school, a couple years younger than my father, but Harry never graduated from high school. Nevertheless, Harry at first worked in construction like his brothers and, at one point, was employed as a television tower installer for a couple years.

In his younger years, Harry had some minor run-ins with the law. As a juvenile, he was referred to authorities for hitting a woman in the head with a snowball. In 1955, at age 17, he was fined and had his license suspended for speeding and running a stop sign. The following year, Harry was convicted of driving without a license, and received a suspended sentence. But a short time later, the court ordered him to serve 23 days in the local jail when he violated conditions of his suspended sentence for once again driving without a license. In June 1957, Harry was in jail again following a car accident. On that occasion, while his license was suspended, Harry allowed another person without a license to drive his unregistered car. For that crime, he was ultimately sentenced to serve ten months in prison, a surprisingly harsh sentence for the crime, suggesting there was more to the story than was reported in the paper. In early May 1959, Harry was fined $3 for running another stop sign.

Then, only three days later, at 2:00 a.m. on May 7, 1959, Harry was in an extremely serious car accident. While driving to Sioux City for construction work, he plowed into the rear of a stalled semitruck on a highway outside of Marshalltown. Police determined Harry had been speeding.

Harry suffered a broken leg, and many cuts and contusions all over his body. Most significantly, however, the hood of his car crumpled upon impact, crashing in through his front windshield. It fractured Harry's skull and sliced a gash across his face. One eye was immediately destroyed and he lost the sight in the other eye before he was discharged from the hospital. He was 21 years old, and permanently blind. Thereafter, Harry walked with a white cane and largely became dependent on Social Security payments to cover daily living expenses.

Despite his terrible accident, Harry soon married a local girl, Karen Kephart. Karen was a short, tiny girl. She was only 15 years old and a freshman in high school when she married Harry. But she immediately dropped out of high school because she was pregnant when she got married. In 1960, in smalltown America, pregnant girls didn't attend high school. It wasn't socially acceptable, especially in small, conservative, Iowa towns.

Harry and Karen wed on April 9, 1960, in a small church ceremony at the First Baptist Church in Mount Pleasant. Their child was born about seven months later, on October 27. They named him Monte. His birth was announced on the second page of the *Mount Pleasant News*, along with the births of three other children. Over the next few years, Harry and Karen would have three more children together in rapid succession: Roberta, Donnie, and the youngest, Mickie.

Monte's father drank a lot. He was a regular at the seedy blue-collar bar, located downtown on the west side of the town square. He was often seen walking there, using his white walking cane to make his way. In addition to drinking a lot, Harry was also emotionally and verbally abusive to Monte's mother and to his children, despite or perhaps because of his blindness.

In the late fall of 1967, when Monte was seven years

old, his parents separated. Monte's mother and her children, including Monte, were soon living in a small rental house in the nearby small town of New London. The day after Christmas, four-year-old Donnie was playing with a candle when he lit the house on fire. The family escaped the ensuing inferno without injury, but by the time the fire department arrived, the house was engulfed in flames. The house and its contents were totally destroyed. The Seager family lost all of their possessions, including the kids' Christmas presents. A newspaper article reporting on the fire the following day solicited donated clothing for the family, listing sizes of the various family members.

For a few months after the fire, Monte, his mother, and his siblings were split up with Karen and her kids living with various relatives. By February 1968, Karen and her children were back together again and had moved into another rental house, this time in the nearby tiny town of Rome, Iowa, eight miles due west of Mount Pleasant. The house was a run-down shack and lacked running water. The family used an outhouse for bathroom facilities.

According to a distant relative, shortly after the move to Rome, Karen left all the kids with Harry and took off, never to return. Blind, unemployed, and unable to care for four young kids by himself, Harry contacted the state authorities for help. They took the kids from Harry and placed them all into the foster care system. The children were split up and sent to separate foster homes.

Monte was then in the second grade in school. Soon after the children were taken away, Monte's parents divorced. Monte's mother moved away, eventually ending up in Indiana. Harry, meanwhile, stayed on in Mount Pleasant.

Over the next decade, Monte was placed in a half-dozen foster homes. He lived once with a foster family in nearby Burlington, Iowa. On another occasion, when Monte was in the 5th and 6th grades, he lived with a family in West Point, a few blocks from where Clementine Beavers' mother lived. There's no indication that there was ever any contact between the Beavers and Monte while he lived briefly in that foster home.

Years later, when I interviewed him in prison, Monte talked to me about his time in foster homes. He had many memories of his times with various foster families. He was bitter about being separated from his parents and siblings. But he never claimed that he was ever subject to neglect or abuse; indeed, he spoke somewhat fondly of his time with one foster family whose father was a medical doctor.

None of Monte's foster placements lasted for long. Monte generally performed well academically, but he often got into trouble outside of school. While living with his foster family in West Point, for example, Monte set a garage on fire. Monte was briefly sent to the mental health institute in Mount Pleasant for evaluation and treatment after that. From there, he was sent to another foster home. That placement didn't last long, either.

By 1976, Monte was living with yet another foster family in Indianola, Iowa, a small town south of Des Moines. He was 15 years old. He joined the middle school

ROTC there where he learned how to shoot a rifle. Monte was continuing to do well in school, earning a B average. Nevertheless, in March of that year, Monte ran away from his foster home. He soon set up a tent in a wooded area near the railroad tracks.

Then on March 30, 1976, Monte hid behind a stack of boxes in the back storeroom of a sporting goods store and waited for all the employees to leave at the end of the day. When the employees eventually closed the store and everyone left the building, Monte emerged from his hiding spot and began to gather up some goods. He loaded a .22 caliber Ruger rifle, 1,300 rounds of ammunition, a rifle scope, a BB handgun, and some other accessories into a bag and slipped out the back door. He took all his stolen goods back to his campsite. It was there that the police found Monte and the stolen merchandise a few days later. The police took Monte into custody and referred him to juvenile services.

Soon after, Monte was convicted of the heist as a juvenile. The judge did not send Monte to a juvenile incarceration facility, but did place Monte on juvenile probation. Monte's latest foster family refused to take him back after this episode, so the state sent Monte to the Iowa Children and Family Services group home for troubled teens in Des Moines. Monte didn't stay there long.

In January 1978, Monte was arrested again, this time for stealing a car. In February, he was charged with possession of stolen property, taken from several break-ins of homes and cars. Monte was now 17 years old. For these crimes, Monte spent a few days in jail, then the court again placed him on juvenile probation.

At this point, the state authorities concluded it was time to send Monte back to his family. During the 1970s, the foster care system across America came under pressure to restructure. The foster care system as envisioned in the 1950s and 1960s contemplated children being placed for short, temporary stays with foster families with a return to the biological parents as soon as possible. But it became apparent, as in Monte's case, that all too often the foster placements lasted years, with children floating from one home to the next. Research had begun to show how detrimental it was for child development for children to be removed for such long periods from their biological parents, while experiencing little stability in residence. So by the late 1970s, increased emphasis was placed on biological parents to take responsibility for their children.

In Monte's case, there was a question of whether he should be returned to his mother or his father. His mother had never visited Monte in any of his foster homes since she left the family a decade ago. But Monte's father had come to see Monte a couple times while he was in the group home. Harry had recently expressed to the state authorities an interest in having him back. Harry had met a woman years before named Sharon Gaylord. By 1970, they began living together in Mount Pleasant. Sharon had a job and a car and, with her help, Harry thought he was equal to the task of taking care of Monte.

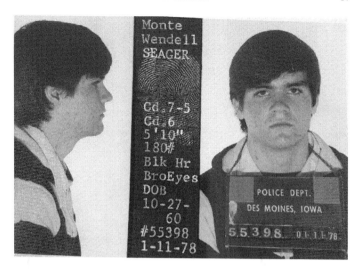

Monte Seager (photo by author from police file)

Nevertheless, the authorities were at first inclined to have Monte's mother take custody of him. The presumption then was that the mother was the natural choice for raising children. Monte's mother was living in Fort Wayne, Indiana by this time. She had remarried to a man name Shields. Karen had just recently taken on the responsibility of caring for her daughter, Roberta, who had also been recently released from foster care. Karen told the authorities that she had her hands full with her daughter and couldn't take care of Monte, too. So, the state concluded it had no choice but to send Monte to live with his father instead. In 1978, Monte's father Harry was 40 years old.

Thus it was that on March 27, 1978, Monte moved to Mount Pleasant to live with his blind father. Monte enrolled as a sophomore in Mount Pleasant High School mid-semester, that spring of 1978. He would turn 18 in October, early in his junior year of high school, about six months after moving in with his father and Sharon Gaylord. Monte's schooling had been interrupted several times due to movements between foster and group homes, so he was a year or two older than most students in his class. To other students, it was as if Monte just appeared from nowhere; no one knew him or knew much about him.

Monte, who hadn't lived with his father since he was seven years old, was now only a few months from legally becoming an adult. Harry had never really raised Monte; in many ways, he barely knew his own son. Now, Harry was responsible for a rebellious teenager, less than a year away from turning 18, who had a significant criminal record already and was on probation. Within seven months of moving in with his father, Monte would kill.

Monte's two younger brothers, Donnie and Mickie, remained in foster care. Mickie was eventually adopted by his foster family and essentially disappeared from the Seager family. Donnie, now 14 years old in 1978, lived with a foster family in Keokuk, Iowa, about a 45-minute drive away from Mount Pleasant, in the Southeast corner of the state. Donnie was allowed to spend occasional weekends with his father in Mount Pleasant; about every other weekend in 1978. On a couple occasions, Karen would come for a visit from Indiana, bringing Monte's sister, Roberta, along so the children could maintain some contact. But Monte's mother and sister never stayed the night when they visited Mount Pleasant.

Harry's live-in girlfriend, Sharon, considered herself to be Harry's common law wife and Monte's stepmother. Monte lived with his father and Sharon at 501 South Jefferson Street in a house his father had inherited a few years before when Monte's grandmother passed away. It was an old, rundown, one and a half story wood frame house, about a block away from a cemetery. The local police were familiar with the Seager residence, having responded to multiple calls for domestic disturbances there over the years. My family had lived up the street on the other side of the road from Monte's house; we moved out of the neighborhood about the time Harry Seager moved in. The Seager home no longer exists; there is now only an empty lot where the house once stood.

The Seager home was situated about four blocks west of the Beavers' home, less than a third of a mile away. The Seager home sat at the bottom of a slight valley between two hills. Between the Seager and Beavers' homes, there was a hill of about 100 feet in height that crested about a block east of the Seager home. The land plateaued then for another block or so before descending back down another gentle valley. The Beavers' home was located about halfway up the next small hill to the east; Lincoln Elementary School sat near the crest of that hill. It would take only five or six minutes for a man walking at a normal pace to cover the distance from one house to the other. Someone running could cover the distance in half that time.

When at home, Monte spent a lot of time watching

television. Monte frequently watched TV for hours on end, often until it went off the air in the wee hours of the morning. Back then, before the time of cable and satellite TV, there was only broadcast television. The signals went off the air around 1:00 or 2:00 in the morning. Meanwhile, Harry would spend many of his evenings listening to the radio in the kitchen, or drinking uptown in the seedy bar on the west side of the town square. Sharon worked the night shift at a local factory.

Monte's relationship with his father was, at best, strained. Monte's father still drank a lot both at home and in the downtown bar. He tended to blame Monte for anything that went wrong. Monte's stepmother Sharon believed Harry often blamed Monte for a lot of things that Donnie did.

Monte didn't have his own car. On rare occasions, Monte was allowed to borrow the one car his stepmother owned. Monte worked various part-time jobs in town and saved up some money, but never enough to buy his own car.

On May 17, 1978, Monte and his stepmother walked uptown a few blocks to the Coast-to-Coast hardware store. Monte said he wanted to buy a gun to shoot for target practice and, because he was only 17, he needed an adult to purchase the firearm. Once in the store, Monte looked over the small selection of firearms and picked out a Mossberg .22 caliber bolt-action rifle to purchase. The weapon had a five-bullet magazine that inserted into the bottom of the stock. After firing the weapon, a new bullet could be chambered from the magazine by pulling back the bolt and ejecting the shell casing; the spring in the magazine automatically chambered a new round. The clerk told him the weapon could fire both .22 shorts and longs, though Monte later concluded that the .22 caliber short shells, sometimes referred to as non-magnum shells, often jammed when attempting to eject them. Monte's stepmother, Sharon, took the cash from Monte and handed it over to the clerk, purchasing the weapon for Monte.

When Monte's little brother Donnie visited, Monte and he often took Monte's rifle to the town dump, located on the far side of Saunders Park, a dozen or so blocks east of the Seager home. There, the two of them would shoot at paper targets thumbtacked to support poles of an abandoned railroad trestle. Sometimes their stepmother Sharon would drive the boys to the park to shoot; other times Monte and Donnie would walk there, carrying the rifle disassembled in an old Army duffle bag that Monte had obtained when he was briefly in the middle school ROTC program in Indianola. At first, Monte and Donnie used the ammunition magazine that came with the weapon when they shot the rifle. But the magazine soon broke and wouldn't feed bullets into the weapon properly. After the magazine broke, they had to load the weapon one bullet at time. After discharging a round, one had to pull back on the bolt, discharge the empty cartridge, insert a new bullet into the chamber by hand, and slide the bolt forward and over to lock it in place before discharging the next round. The process of reloading typically took 30-40 seconds. They never practiced speed loading, but through repetition they became more adept at doing it rapidly.

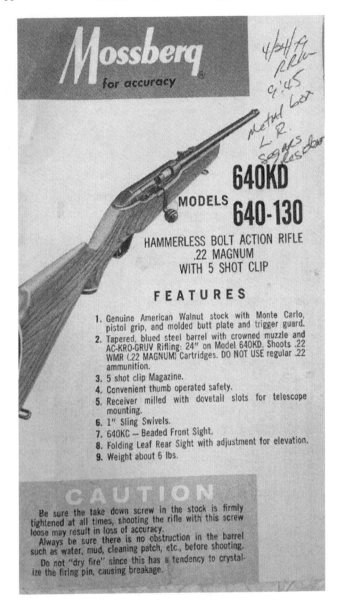

Mossberg
for accuracy

MODELS **640KD**
640-130

HAMMERLESS BOLT ACTION RIFLE
.22 MAGNUM
WITH 5 SHOT CLIP

F E A T U R E S

1. Genuine American Walnut stock with Monte Carlo, pistol grip, and molded butt plate and trigger guard.
2. Tapered, blued steel barrel with crowned muzzle and AC-KRO-GRUV Rifling: 24″ on Model 640KD. Shoots .22 WMR (.22 MAGNUM) Cartridges. DO NOT USE regular .22 ammunition.
3. 5 shot clip Magazine.
4. Convenient thumb operated safety.
5. Receiver milled with dovetail slots for telescope mounting.
6. 1″ Sling Swivels.
7. 640KC — Beaded Front Sight.
8. Folding Leaf Rear Sight with adjustment for elevation.
9. Weight about 6 lbs.

C A U T I O N

Be sure the take down screw in the stock is firmly tightened at all times, shooting the rifle with this screw loose may result in loss of accuracy.
Always be sure there is no obstruction in the barrel such as water, mud, cleaning patch, etc., before shooting.
Do not "dry fire" since this has a tendency to crystallize the firing pin, causing breakage.

Instruction Manual (photo by author of manual in police file)

Aside from target shooting at the dump, Monte would on occasion also take his gun out at night on his own and go to McMillan Park. McMillan Park was a large 40-acre city park, home to the Midwest Old Threshers Reunion grounds and the Henry County Fairgrounds. In the park there were grandstands, a dirt track, and scores of buildings, large and small. At the park, Monte liked to shoot out the street lights because the mercury vapor lightbulbs would explode when hit by bullets. He enjoyed watching them explode.

Like the Beavers, the Seagers were also Catholic. Unlike the Beavers, the Seagers rarely attended church. Monte's stepmother later speculated that Monte would have embraced religion a little more if someone would have attended church with him. But that seldom occurred.

Monte was of average height (about 5 feet, ten inches), but with a slight frame. He wore his black hair long, shoulder-length, and it was his pride. But he had a bad complexion with severe acne and pockmark scars on his face. Monte was generally reclusive, a loner. "Quiet" was the adjective fellow students most often used to describe Monte. He seldom talked to anyone and didn't interact with others. Some thought him "odd" or "weird." But Monte could be quick to smile on occasion and seemed pleasant enough when he wanted to be, particularly with teachers he liked. His school photo in the high school yearbook for his junior year shows him smiling pleasantly enough at the camera lens.

Monte Seager (photo by author from Mount Pleasant High School Yearbook)

Monte wasn't part of the popular crowd at school. His small clique of associates were the students who, like him, smoked cigarettes and weed. But he was not generally a trouble maker in school and didn't have many disciplinary problems. His grades were below average when he attended Mount Pleasant High School, which contrasted sharply with his grades in middle school when he received mostly A's and B's. Indeed, a later IQ test would show that Monte had a combined IQ of 123; in the superior intelligence range.

In high school in Mount Pleasant, Monte didn't participate in sports or other extracurricular activities. He once thought about going out for football his junior year, but didn't pay attention to when practice started in August, so had already missed a month of practice by the time he looked into it. I was on the football team, playing linebacker. Monte would have had a hard time fitting in with the other members of the team, given his background. But there were a couple other smokers who had gone out for football, the kind of people Monte hung around with, and by the end of the season they were integrated team members. It might have done a lot of good had Monte joined the team. But he didn't join the football team or any other team sport.

Occasionally, Monte attended school events, like football games, but when he did so he usually went alone. The one extracurricular activity Monte engaged in was joining the Target staff. "Target" was the name ironically given to the high school yearbook. Monte had become interested in photography years before and had some experience. He was assigned the task of being one of the yearbook staff photographers.

Monte didn't have a lot of friends, being new to both Mount Pleasant and the school. The guys he hung out with, like Dennis Cornell and Bill Snyder, were some of the smokers on the corner, guys who, like Monte, smoked marijuana and had minor scrapes with the law. Monte didn't date any girls. He never had a girlfriend. Indeed, he didn't seem to others to have any interest in girls.

Monte was assigned to a locker with another student in my class, Charlie Vestweber, who similarly had just recently moved to town. They were assigned locker 252, on the second floor of the high school, near the typing room. Other than being assigned as locker mates, Monte and Charlie had little in common and had little interaction with each other. Charlie was a sophomore, in my grade, while Monte was a junior. They didn't share any classes together. Charlie, a genuinely outgoing and friendly guy, tried to engage with Monte when, on occasion, they met up at their locker. But Monte seemingly made no effort to befriend his locker mate. Monte would talk only when spoken to. Otherwise, he was quiet. Quiet, perhaps a little odd; that was the view of Monte Seager in the fall of 1978.

It was generally known through the rumor mill in high school that Monte had been in trouble with the law, having allegedly engaged in petty thefts and other crimes. The details were unknown and the subject of speculation among students. School authorities knew that Monte was on juvenile probation. The teachers had the right to review his probation file, but most chose not to do so; they didn't want to prejudge him.

I personally saw little of Monte at first. I didn't have

any classes with him. Occasionally, I saw him in the hallways of the high school. More often I saw him when I walked to my car after school. To reach my car in the parking lot after school, I had to pass by Monte and the other students smoking cigarettes on the sidewalk just off the school property where the school couldn't do anything about it. I remember feeling intimidated by him, a little scared of getting beat up by him or one of the other kids he hung out with. But Monte never threatened me or anyone else that I know of. I guess he just looked mean.

As it happened, Monte Seager and Karol Beavers shared a speech class together that fall of 1978. The class was taught by Marilyn Vincent, a young teacher who also directed the drama department. Ms. Vincent thought Monte was generally a positive person and talkative with other students, an observation that contrasts with the students' universal description of Monte as quiet. She noted that fall of 1978 that Monte was quick to smile, was polite, and seemed well-groomed.

Marilyn Vincent (photo taken by Monte Seager contained in police file)

There were a total of 14 students in the class, including Monte and Karol, ten of whom were girls. Karol sat in the front row, near the door. Monte sat three rows away, on the north wall. Monte would have walked by Karol every time he came into the room. He and Karol were observed by others to chat with each other sometimes in class, but not often, and not about anything that was noteworthy. Monte never asked Karol out on a date, tried to walk her to her next class, or make any other advance toward her to anyone's knowledge. Monte would later tell investigators that he thought Karol was good looking and had a nice personality. And he didn't think she was a flirt, except with Lance Poock. Monte would later tell me when I interviewed him in prison for this book that he didn't know Karol well and never asked her out, but, he assured me, that once "we locked eyes."

On October 10, 1978, Monte gave a speech in class about his hobby, photography. He brought four cameras to class and told his fellow students about the cameras, described their operation, and explained how he developed the film. One of the cameras was a Polaroid and, as part of his speech, he took photos of some of the students and handed the photos out to the students when they instantly developed.

The speech went over well. Monte clearly enjoyed talking about his hobby and the students thought it great fun to get photos of themselves. During the next two weeks following his speech, Monte brought a camera to class often and took photos of other students. He mostly took photos of the girls, though, Ms. Vincent noticed. Monte took several photos of Karol and her friends, Lisa Howe and Cathy Whaley. After he developed the film, Monte would bring the photos to class and give copies to the girls.

Ms. Vincent thought Monte's interest in photography was a good thing for him. In her opinion, Monte lacked self-confidence. His photography, and providing students with copies of his photos, resulted in a lot of positive attention for him from the other students, she noted. Ms.

Vincent considered it generous of Monte to hand out photos to his fellow students. She didn't recall seeing any developed photos Monte took of Karol alone, or where she was the focus of the image.

But there were. Monte took several black and white photos of Karol. Karol was excited about getting copies of the photos and continuously asked Monte when they would be ready. He gave her several, some of which she put on a mirror in her bedroom.

Monte took one photograph of Karol while she presented a speech in class, just a few weeks before she died. Karol's speech was about babysitting. She brought her infant nephew to class as part of her speech. In the photo Monte took of Karol during her speech, she is sitting erect behind a desk. Karol is smiling brightly, looking off to her left, likely in response to something Ms. Vincent had said to her about the speech. Her right hand rests protectively on the back of her nephew who is crawling on the desktop. The joy Karol felt at the moment, and her sense of humor, can be read in her expression. Also apparent in the photograph is the heart-shaped necklace her mother had given her for her 16th birthday the previous April. The necklace she always wore.

Karol Beavers and her nephew Christopher in speech class, October 1978 (photo taken by Monte Seager, contained in police file)

Apparently unaware of the identity of the photographer, the Target staff ironically chose that photo of Karol for a memorial page to her in the 1979 yearbook.

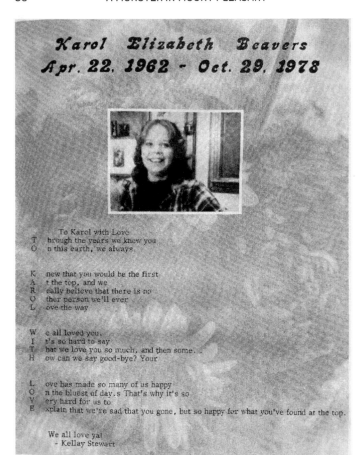

Karol Elizabeth Beavers
Apr. 22, 1962 - Oct. 29, 1978

To Karol with Love
T hrough the years we knew you
O n this earth, we always

K new that you would be the first
A t the top, and we
R eally believe that there is no
O ther person we'll ever
L ove the way

W e all loved you,
I t's so hard to say
T hat we love you so much, and then some. . .
H ow can we say good-bye? Your

L ove has made so many of us happy
O n the bluest of day.s That's why it's so
V ery hard for us to
E xplain that we're sad that you gone, but so happy for what you've found at the top.

We all love ya!
- Kellay Stewart

Memorial Page from 1979 Target Yearbook (photo by author)

On Friday, October 27, 1978, Monte Seager turned 18 years old. Monte was now an adult. In 1978, the legal drinking age in Iowa was 18. His father bought him a bottle of rum for his birthday present.

SEVEN
THE INITIAL INVESTIGATION

"Skepticism and doubt lead to study and investigation, and investigation is the beginning of wisdom." — Clarence Darrow, Why I Am an Agnostic and Other Essays

EVENTUALLY, A TOTAL OF SIX STATE BCI AGENTS arrived in Mount Pleasant to assist local law enforcement officers. The out-of-town agents took up temporary residency to pursue leads in the Beavers' murder case, working alongside the Mount Pleasant Police Department and the Henry County Sheriff's Office. BCI Special Agent Larry Goepel was placed in charge of the overall investigation.

The BCI agents stayed in town for months working on the case. The government housed them at the Iris Motel on the west side of town, adjacent to the Iris Restaurant. At night, the agents often ate in the attached restaurant, always sitting at the same large round table, and they frequented the restaurant's lounge. In the lounge, a bright and pretty, but reserved, cocktail waitress in her early thirties, named Sue Wheelock, waited on them from time to time. Whether she would soon die depended on the success of their investigation. But neither she, nor the agents, knew that at the time.

The agents fanned out in Mount Pleasant and interviewed everybody that had even the slightest connection to the Beavers. Agents received all kinds of potential leads. In the months that followed the murders, many people suddenly thought they saw something the night of the murders, or recalled some strange man or unfamiliar vehicle in town around the time of the murders. Though immediately after the murders there were no such leads, with time people began to remember, or imagined they remembered, weird events or odd happenings or suspicious people. This was the product of honest people racking their brains for anything that may have seemed out of line, anything that may produce even the smallest lead. The agents diligently checked out every tip they received, interviewing scores of people, no matter how implausible the lead might have been. Nothing panned out. Nothing tied back to the Beavers' murders.

The agents kept at it, though, striving diligently to solve the Beavers' murders, running down every lead they had, every thread they found, every possibility they could think of, no matter how unlikely. Agents looked up the TV Guide to double check Max's recollection of the television program playing when he claimed he went to bed, and turned on the TV in the basement to see if it was, in fact, tuned to that channel. Agents stopped into every shoe store in town, including my dad's Corner Cobbler, with a photo of the bloody shoeprints from the garage floor, checking the back of the shoes trying to determine the make and style of shoe that left the prints, then checking suspects for whether they owned that type of shoe, only later to discover the prints were made by one of the investigating police officers.

The agents considered the possibility that the three men who installed the new carpet in the Beavers' basement the Friday before the murders might have had something to do with the murders. They tracked down each one, ran their criminal histories, and interviewed them. The agents noted that all three men were married, seemingly happily so, none had a criminal record, and their stories all checked out.

Officers traveled to every hotel in the area and inspected the registers for any out-of-town visitors, and then investigated the backgrounds and criminal histories of the patrons. Nothing about these visitors to Mount Pleasant led anywhere. Officers followed up on reports of any transients in the neighborhood. They collected lists of every inmate on work release in the area. They solicited lists from other law enforcement departments around the area of the so-called usual suspects; people who had prior run-ins with the law. The agents researched whether there were any other murders in the Midwest around the same time and followed up to see if the suspects in any of those murders could possibly be linked to the Beavers. Agents even searched nearby bodies of water and rivers with a scuba diver hoping to find a ditched murder weapon or clothes, all with negative results. Nothing checked out. Nothing materialized. Leads led to dead ends.

At one point the agents thought they had a particularly promising lead. A teenage runaway from Illinois had stolen a car from a house in a town not far from Mount Pleasant a few days before the murders. When he was caught a few days later in Texas, the police found a .22 caliber bullet in the car. Agents traveled to Texas to interview the suspect and spent hours doing so, tracing the bullet, checking out the kid's story. But it, like every other lead, went absolutely nowhere.

Suspicion initially fell on Max, of course. He was, after all, the only person home at the time of the murders. Some people understandably found it hard to believe that he slept through the murders of his wife and daughter. The police determined Max had not taken sleeping pills. Given that his deep sleep wasn't drug induced, it seemed implausible that he didn't wake up to the gunshots that took place just down the hall from his bedroom. So it was incomprehensible to many, even to many law enforcement officers, that Max didn't have something to do with the murders. Indeed, the BCI agents who descended upon Mount Pleasant were at first convinced that Max had committed the murders.

But Max had absolutely no violence in his history, was a loving husband and father, and had no motive to kill his wife and daughter. He also was a little hard of hearing, being almost deaf in one ear, which would explain why he didn't hear anything the night of the murders. Further, it was absolutely inconceivable that he would rape his own daughter. Max volunteered to take a lie detector test and passed it without a hitch.

Those who really knew Max, like Mount Pleasant Chief of Police Gus Hagers, knew there was no way Max committed the murders. Gus had known Max for years. He shopped at Max's grocery store. They golfed together. He knew Max personally. Although Gus conceded that any man could conceivably become angry enough to kill his wife, perhaps even Max, it was impossible to contemplate that he raped and killed his own daughter. It took days for the local officers to convince the BCI agents that Max had not committed the murders. Suspicion that Max killed his wife and daughter was finally and completely put to rest when testing showed that Max's blood type didn't match that of the semen found in his daughter or the saliva found on her breast.

Despite interviewing scores of people, no one seemingly was aware of anyone who would have been out to harm the Beavers. Indeed, they were considered some of the nicest people in town. Max told the police he wasn't aware of anyone who was upset or angry with him, or for that matter anyone who was angry with any other member of the family. The Beavers had no known enemies, he declared. He hadn't had any business disputes with anyone, and he didn't owe anyone a lot of money; just typical ongoing business accounts payable. Max could think of no one and no reason to kill his wife and young daughter.

Nevertheless, there was still some speculation that

perhaps someone angry with Max killed his wife and daughter. This theory rested on the circuitous notion that Max was somehow connected to organized crime in Chicago and the murders were in retaliation for skimming money from the mob. This conjecture arose from the death of another Mount Pleasant businessman just a few years before.

Late on a night in September 1975, Walter Wellington died in an explosion behind a Mount Pleasant bank. It appeared that Wellington was attempting to place a home-made bomb made of dynamite near the back door of the bank when it went off. Parts of his body were later found a half-block away. My mother had been called out that night, like she later was with the Beavers' murders, to take photos at the crime scene.

Wellington was a used car dealer, but it also turned out that he was part of a stolen car ring headed by Chicago gangsters. The rumor in that case was that Wellington was skimming from the mob and was killed by them. But the police concluded that Wellington was killed while he attempted to rob the bank either so he could get cash to pay back the mobsters, or in an effort to distract criminal investigators who were focusing on his business dealings.

So when more violence occurred in our quiet and peaceful town of Mount Pleasant, some naturally remembered the Wellington case and speculated that Max was somehow connected to the ring. Perhaps, it was speculated, Max was involved with Wellington, owed the Chicago gangsters money like Wellington did, and so the gangsters killed his wife and daughter. It took some time for this theory to die out. Even a cursory investigation showed Max had no connections to used cars, mobsters from Chicago, or the Wellingtons. There was, in short, nothing to connect Max with anything like what Walt Wellington was involved in.

Officers also searched for a motive for killing Karol. They interviewed many students and took fingerprints from a few males, like Lance Poock and Brad Gardner, who were believed to be close to or romantically involved with Karol. At one point, they had all the students who worked on the homecoming float in Karol's garage the week before her murder gather in a classroom at the high school. The officers solicited those students for any information they might have about the murders or who would have wanted to harm Karol. The officers wanted to know if anything suspicious occurred or whether anything was said or done that would give a clue as to the murderer. None of the students had noticed anything suspicious. None had any insight. No strange boys were there that night, and no one had said or done anything to suggest they had an issue with Karol. None of the students had anything of value to offer the officers.

Officers interviewed Karol's closest friends, Lisa Howe and Cathy Whaley and others, but they, too, had little information to offer. They didn't know of any boy Karol had spurned or of anyone who would have been out to harm her for any reason. Karol had never mentioned to her friends that she was afraid of any boy or of anyone else. Karol wasn't known for sleeping around or making out with other girls' boyfriends. She wasn't involved in drug use and didn't get in trouble with the law. Her friends were the studious, clean, uncomplicated types. Karol simply had no known enemies.

There was no evidence of a jealous lover or jilted boyfriend. Karol's closest friends didn't think Karol had been sexually active with her ex-boyfriend, Brad Gardner, or with anyone else and felt confident that Karol would have told them if she had been sexually active. Officers nevertheless checked with the local Planned Parenthood office, but it had no records of Karol ever obtaining birth control pills from the organization.

Karol's most recent boyfriend, Brad Gardner, had an airtight alibi as well and was quickly eliminated as a suspect. Brad was with his new girlfriend and her parents the night of the murders. Further, when Brad's blood type didn't come back as O positive, it clearly eliminated him as a suspect.

From speaking with other students, law enforcement officers came to understand that Karol was very popular and that many boys had asked her out. Officers learned that Karol had turned down several boys who had asked her out, but she was said to have done so gently. The officers didn't discover any boy who was angry with her. She wasn't "stuck up," as the phrase was used back then. But she was selective in who she dated.

Officers learned that one boy, Chuck Ganka, had once persuaded his twelve-year-old sister to deliver flowers to Karol's house one time. Chuck instructed his sister to knock on Karol's bedroom window and tell Karol that Chuck had picked the flowers for Karol. Despite the romantic gesture, Karol had turned Chuck down when he later asked her out. Agents interviewed Chuck. He wasn't angry about being turned down, he assured them. When the agents investigated where Chuck was the night of the murders, they learned Chuck had a solid alibi. So that lead went nowhere, just like every other lead.

Desperate for any possible leads, officers contacted the district's juvenile probation officer to obtain a list of all juvenile males on probation. The police officers quizzed the probation officer about what she knew about each person on the list. The officers then followed up with each person named on the list to find out if there was any violence in their criminal histories, where they were the night of the murders, and if they had any connection to the Beavers.

Monte Seager's name was on the list. The probation officer told investigators that Monte had a fairly extensive juvenile record involving some thefts, burglaries, and arsons. The probation officer also mentioned that Monte had recently been evaluated at the Mental Health Institute in Mount Pleasant. The probation officer explained that she had talked with Monte fairly recently. The conversation focused on Monte's need to become more social. The probation officer had encouraged Monte to date girls. The probation officer said that Monte told her that all the waitresses at his job at the Iris Restaurant were sluts and didn't wear bras. The probation officer opined that, based on her conversations with Monte, she didn't think Monte was sexually active.

Officers obtained class records for Monte from Mount

Pleasant High School and compared the list of classes he attended against Karol's. They saw that Monte and Karol both attended the same speech class. Officers followed up by asking some of Karol's classmates from speech class about any connection between Monte and Karol. The students all reported that Karol was nice to Monte and would say hi to him, but that was really all the interaction they seemed to have. Students told the officers about Monte taking photos of Karol and others in the class. Karol's closest friends said that Karol never mentioned anything about being concerned or afraid of Monte, or that he had ever bothered her.

Nevertheless, officers initially looked at Monte as a possible suspect, too. Officers investigated where Monte was the day of the Beavers' murders. Through interviewing various people, officers learned that Monte's brother, Donnie, had come to Mount Pleasant for a visit the weekend of the murders. On Saturday the 28th of October, Monte, Donnie, and their father went out for lunch with Donnie driving. They were celebrating Monte's 18th birthday. Donnie reported that Monte and Harry were drinking in the car. They returned back home mid-afternoon and stayed home the rest of the night. The following day, Monte worked the lunch shift as the fry chef at the Iris Restaurant, leaving about 10:00 in the morning, and getting home around 2:00 or 2:30 that same afternoon. Sharon drove Donnie back to his foster family in Keokuk sometime later that afternoon; Monte rode along. Sharon and Monte arrived back home around dinner time. It wasn't clear from the initial interviews what Monte did the rest of that Sunday evening, the night of the murders.

So, on Thursday, November 2, 1978, a BCI agent and Chief Hagers interviewed Monte while he was at work at the Iris Restaurant. Chief Hagers entered the restaurant and asked Monte if he was willing to talk with the police. Monte readily agreed and followed Chief Hagers outside. The Chief and the BCI agent questioned Monte while the three of them sat in Chief Hagers' squad car. It was a short interview, lasting only about 15 to 20 minutes.

The officers asked Monte what he knew of the Beavers' murders. Monte claimed he knew nothing about the murders. Monte professed that he learned about the murders only second-hand, when he was handing in a speech in class. He claimed that when he approached the teacher another student was there. Monte explained he overheard the other student telling the teacher about the murders. The officers didn't confront Monte at the time with how his story about learning of the murders conflicted with Ms. Vincent's version.

Monte explained that he worked at the Iris Restaurant that Sunday morning of the murders, but said he was back home by mid-afternoon. Officers later checked the time cards at the restaurant and confirmed this was accurate.

The officers asked Monte about his relationship with Karol. Monte admitted knowing Karol from school, but denied having any attachment to her and claimed he had no idea where she lived at the time of the murders. He mentioned, however, that several days after the murders he was with a friend who drove by the house and pointed it out to Monte; there was still police tape stretched around the property. But Monte declared that was the only way he found out where Karol lived.

The officers asked Monte if he owned any firearms. He readily admitted that he owned a .22 caliber rifle. He explained he shot at targets with it. Monte exclaimed that he never hunted with the rifle because he didn't like killing animals. The BCI agent asked Monte if he owned any handguns, and Monte answered no. Chief Hagers inquired whether Monte would let the officers examine his rifle and Monte said he would. But after the interview, the BCI agent told Chief Hagers there was no reason to go retrieve Monte's rifle. The agent didn't seem interested in Monte's rifle, still assuming the murderer used a revolver.

The officers quizzed Monte about where he was the night of the Beavers' murders. Monte stated he was at home that night and never left the house. Monte claimed he was watching television shows that evening. He recalled first watching *Battlestar Galactica*, which he explained he always watched on Sunday evenings. Then he said he recalled watching a movie about an airplane crash in a Florida swamp.[1] Monte claimed he went to bed at about 10:00 p.m.

---

1. The movie was called *The Ghost of Flight 401*, and it aired for the first time in 1978. The movie tells the story of an aircraft that crashed in the Florida Everglades, killing 103 passengers; 75 passengers and crew survived. After the wreckage was removed, salvageable parts from the plane were used to repair other aircraft. Soon passengers and crew on those aircraft reported seeing what they believed to be the ghost of the wrecked airplane's flight engineer. The movie was based on the true story

As it happened, Chief Hagers had watched that same movie about the airplane crash that same evening. This was back in the day of broadcast television, when one couldn't record programs on tapes or CDs or stream programs. The show came on the television and you either sat down and watched it when it was broadcast or you missed it.

Knowing what happened in the movie from watching it himself, Chief Hagers cross-examined Monte about the movie. Monte was able to recite quite a bit of detail about the airplane crash movie, accurately describing the plot and the rest of the movie. Monte's knowledge of the show persuaded the officers that Monte must have been home watching the movie just as he claimed. So after talking with Monte for about 15 minutes, they let him go back to work.

After talking with Monte, the officers drove to his house to interview Monte's parents. Monte's stepmother, Sharon, was able to partially corroborate Monte's alibi, saying that she saw him at home at 10:00 p.m. She explained that her mother called about 10:00 p.m. and Monte answered the phone. Sharon asserted that she believed Monte went to bed after answering the phone and she didn't see Monte again after that. Sharon left for work at 10:40 p.m. (she worked the night shift starting at

---

of an airplane crash in 1972, the salvaging of parts from the plane, and stories of passengers of planes using those parts who claimed to have seen ghosts. This was typical of the horror and disaster movies popular in the 1970s.

11:00 p.m. at a local factory), she explained, and was sure Monte was in bed asleep when she left for work.

Monte's father, Harry, confirmed that Monte was home watching TV most of the night. Harry mentioned that he thought he heard Monte go out of the house after Sharon left for work, but didn't recall hearing Monte come back into the house. Being blind, he couldn't of course say that he saw Monte anywhere and didn't claim to have talked to Monte that evening. Harry stated he was listening to the radio in the kitchen for a bit that evening while he could hear Monte watching TV in the next room. And then Harry said he went to bed. Harry admitted he could have just been asleep when Monte came back into the house.

Harry and Sharon mentioned that Monte often stayed up late watching TV. They both said Monte would often watch shows on TV until the stations went off the air in the early morning hours.

After interviewing Monte, his father, and his step-mother, the officers didn't have much reason to view Monte as a strong suspect. He had a decent alibi of being home watching a movie during the time the officers believed the Beavers were murdered, and his parents partially corroborated that alibi. Monte didn't seem to have any particular connection to Karol. And, although he owned a firearm, it wasn't a revolver which, at that time, the officers were fairly convinced was the type of weapon the killer used. So, the officers moved on to consider other possible suspects.

Among them were Monte's friend Dennis Cornell, and

Monte's little brother, Donnie. Cornell was a known associate of Monte's and a local troublemaker. Cornell was arrested in 1977 for burglary and sent to the Iowa Training School for Boys in Eldora, Iowa. Officers obtained fingerprints, blood samples, and pubic hairs from these two boys, as they did from other possible suspects. The analysis all came up negative as to matching anything at the crime scene. None of the fingerprints came back as matching Cornell or Donnie, they didn't have O-positive blood, and the hairs didn't match. Likewise, officers were quickly able to eliminate Cornell as a suspect because he had an airtight and reliable alibi; he was in juvenile custody at the Boys Home in Eldora at the time of the murders.

Officers also ruled out Donnie, who was a couple years younger than Monte, because there was no known connection between him and Karol. Donnie lived in a foster home in Keokuk (almost an hour's drive away) and attended a different school. Officers also established Donnie was in Keokuk at the time of the murders, so clearly could not have committed them.

Officers received numerous reports about an "unidentified man," or a man perhaps named Andy Collins, who was allegedly seen in the Beavers' neighborhood the night of the murders. This lead started with the high school athletic director, Bob Evans, who was working late at the high school on that Sunday night of the murders. While working in his office at about 7:00 p.m., he heard someone attempt to enter the high school through several locked doors. When Evans stepped out of his office to investigate, he saw a man walking away from the high school in the general direction of the Beavers' house located a half-dozen blocks to the south. He was wearing a burgundy-colored parka. Evans called out to him, accusingly.

"Hey, what are you doing?" Evans asked.

"Just taking a shortcut," the man answered. He was too far away now for Evans to tell who it was.

"Who are you?" Evans demanded.

"Andy Collins," the man answered as he walked away.

Other witnesses also claimed to see this mysterious man walking in the Beavers' neighborhood wearing a burgundy-colored parka. The man had the hood of the parka pulled over his head, so witnesses had little to offer about the man's facial features. This man was suspicious in part because the heavy parka seemed greater protection against the cold than was called for by the unseasonably warm weather that evening. The Andy Collins lead went nowhere, though; officers were never able to identify anyone by that name or find the unidentified man in the parka.

Officers also quickly ruled out any connection with the so-called "circuit rapist." In the previous 17 months, eight women had been raped and another nine assaulted in the surrounding communities of Burlington, Iowa City, Cedar Rapids, Davenport, Clinton, and Muscatine. For various reasons, law enforcement authorities believed all of these rapes and attempted sexual assaults were committed by the same man. This crime, the brutal murders of the Beavers, however, had none of the earmarks of that serial rapist and there was no connection of these other rapes to Mount Pleasant.

Eventually, the Iowa BCI reached out to the FBI for help. On November 21, 1978, FBI crime scene experts examined photographs and evidence from the homicides. They compiled a profile, an early version of the psychological profiling that the FBI would later perfect. Based on their analysis, they provided a description of the perpetrator of the Beavers' homicides:

1. White
2. Male
3. 18-30 [years old]
4. Small frame
5. Domineering mother - defensive mother
6. Kills for his own security
7. Seldom or never dates
8. Semi-skilled
9. Nocturnal person
10. Planned homicides
11. Uses own weapon - not a weapon of opportunity
12. Statistics show defendant lives within one-quarter (1/4) mile of scene
13. Masturbates frequently
14. Excites self through use of pornography
15. Borderline schizophrenia
16. Simple schizophrenia (had intercourse)
17. Degraded body by taking to garage near garbage
18. Contact w/Karol on Sunday (visual, personal, etc.)
19. Poor hygiene
20. Known family but not emotional fondness

. . .

OFFICERS WOULD LATER CONCLUDE THAT MONTE FIT 12 of the 20 characteristics described by the FBI agents as fitting the profile of the man who committed the murders. Monte was a white male of the right age, small-framed, had nocturnal habits, seldom if ever dated girls, was semi-skilled (cook, photographer), lived almost within a quarter mile of the Beavers, knew Karol (though there was no evidence Monte had contact with her, even from afar, that Sunday), had acne and poor hygiene, and didn't have a close family relationship or fondness, having grown up mostly in foster homes. Several of the profile characteristics described the killer, whoever he was (planned homicides, used own weapon, borderline schizophrenic based on having sex with the dead or dying victim, degraded the body), and frankly didn't narrow down suspects at all. It's not clear that the agents ever looked into Monte's mother's parenting style or his masturbation history. But other than Monte matching some of the characteristics in the profile, the officers had nothing else to really suggest that Monte should be a prime suspect. Or a suspect at all. So he wasn't.

On November 17, 1978, a couple weeks after agents first interviewed him, Monte checked out a book entitled *Crime Scientists* from the Mount Pleasant High School library. Written for consumption by the general public, the book contained chapters describing the information and clues forensic scientists can discover from analyzing blood, and how forensic experts perform ballistics examinations and can make comparisons of markings on bullets to identify weapons used in crimes. Investigators would learn of Monte checking out this book only much later, almost a year later, when another student checked out the same book, noticed Monte's name, and told a teacher, who then contacted the police. By then, however, Monte had killed again.

EIGHT

"THE MOOD HERE IS DARK, SOMBER"

"Nothing beats a haunted moonlit night on All Hallows Eve…. And on this fatal night, at this witching time, the starless sky laments black and unmoving. The somber hues of an ominous, dark forest are suddenly illuminated under the emerging face of the full moon." – Elizabeth Kim

IN THE DAYS AND WEEKS AND MONTHS FOLLOWING the murders of Clementine and Karol, the once peaceful town of Mount Pleasant was transformed. Fear prevailed as the overwhelming response and it spread throughout the town. The police continued to have no suspects, no leads, no motive. People were afraid of a killer afoot among them in their small town, wondering if or when he would strike again.

The murders of Clementine and Karol was the leading news story in the local paper, the *Mount Pleasant News*, for weeks on end. The *Mount Pleasant News* was delivered in the afternoon, so by the time it went to press on the first day of the murders the full impact of the murders had been felt. Splashed across the front page above the fold was a photo of the front of the Beavers' home, with the door to the garage ajar.

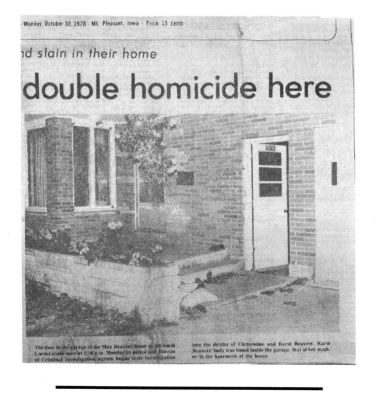

Front page of Mount Pleasant News *on October 30, 1978 (photo by author of clipping of Mount Pleasant News)*

The authorities wouldn't initially reveal to the public or press how the victims were killed. The day after the murders, all the *Mount Pleasant News* could report was that the police had no suspects on the double homicide. A couple days later, the police revealed that the autopsies showed that both victims were shot to death. And that Karol had been sexually assaulted. In the weeks that followed, however, the paper had little more to report.

On the Monday morning after the murders, word spread quickly in the school, but in whispers. The hallways were nearly silent despite the press of students making their way to classrooms between the bells. Stifled sobs could be heard from small groups of girls hugging each other near their lockers. As they passed each other in the hallways on their way to classes, students looked at one another in numb disbelief, searching each other's faces for some sign of hope that it was all just a bad dream. Many students were in a state of shock. Nothing like this had ever happened before. It was, to many of us, inconceivable that one of our classmates could be brutally murdered.

When teacher Marilyn Vincent arrived for school that Monday morning, she hadn't yet heard about the murders. She later recalled that Monte Seager was waiting for her outside her room when she reached it. He followed her into her room. Monte liked Ms. Vincent and would occasionally come to her classroom outside his normal class time. So, she didn't consider his presence outside her classroom that particular morning necessarily unusual. But as she put away her things to prepare for class, Monte asked her if she had heard about the murders. She recalled that he seemed eager to tell her about the murders, almost, she thought, as if he was happy to tell her. At the time, she reasoned that it was simply a case of a person being happy to be in a position to serve as the source of information that someone else didn't know, to share gossip, if you will. In any event, it didn't alarm Ms. Vincent at all at the time, or cause her to question Monte's eagerness to tell her. She, like everyone else, was shocked to hear the tragic news.

On Tuesday morning after the murders, a memorial service was held for Karol in the high school gym. The high school students and teachers gathered together, sitting in the bleachers of the gym where Karol once led crowds in cheers. It's not clear whether Monte was present at the service; no attendance was taken. School records show he was at school that day (though records show he was absent the afternoon of Friday, November 3, and the first three days of the following week of school). So, presumably he sat in the stands with the rest of us, among us.

Despite hundreds of students jammed into the gym, there was very little noise. The mood was subdued; sobbing could be heard in the hushed atmosphere. Karol's priest, Father Albers, conducted the services, along with several ministers of other faiths from the community. The religious leaders solicited God's comfort and support, trying their best to explain the inexplicable, urging those present to take comfort in knowing that Karol and her mother were in a better place. At the end of the service, the high school band, absent one of their flutists, played the *Battle Hymn of the Republic*.

"The Mood Here is Dark, Somber" was the headline splashed across the top of the *Mount Pleasant News* the

Wednesday following the murders. The paper noted that a sense of fear and apprehension pervaded the community. The Mayor of Mount Pleasant, Ed King,[1] asked for trick-or-treating on Halloween that evening be limited to the 1½ hours immediately following sunset, and asked for extra police patrols that night. Hardware stores reported a run on door locks and flashlights. Citizens began locking their doors at night, many for the first time in their lives. Young women no longer ventured out alone, anywhere. Everyone, it seemed, was anxious and on edge, unsure who the killer was that lurked in their midst.

For children in Mount Pleasant, particularly for Karol's fellow high school students, it was the end of an age of innocence. Before Karol and her mother were murdered, we couldn't imagine a world in which we were unsafe. Murders happened in big cities, in bad neighborhoods, typically involving people engaged in criminal activity. People weren't raped and murdered in smalltown Iowa. We couldn't conceive of a fair and just world in which an innocent girl and her mother could be slaughtered, in which someone would violate that sweet, laughing classmate's young body. We were confronted with the ugly reality that tragic things could happen to people

---

1. Ed King would himself be murdered less than ten years later. On December 10, 1986, while Mayor King presided over a city council meeting, a 69-year-old World War II veteran, disgruntled and angry about a sewer backing up in his home, burst into the meeting brandishing a small caliber revolver. He approached the city council bench and gunned down the mayor, shooting him at near point-blank range in the head. The man wounded several other council members until he ran out of bullets and was wrestled to the ground.

who did nothing to deserve it, who didn't place themselves in harm's way, who didn't flirt with danger or associate with evil people. Gone were the days of coming home from school to empty houses oblivious to the danger that potentially lay within. Never again would the students of Mount Pleasant High see the world in the same innocent light, or breathe the air with the same sense of freedom and safety. Those days were gone for good.

On Wednesday evening, the junior girls had been scheduled to play against the senior girls in the traditional Mount Pleasant High School Powder Puff game at the Maple Leaf Athletic Complex. It was a highlight of the fall football season that the students and their parents loved to watch. Karol had been an enthusiastic member of the junior class team. She had practiced hard for the game. School officials cancelled it.

The Thursday morning Des Moines Register quoted a neighbor of the Beavers as saying: "We're frightened. This is something you think can't happen here, but it did—and to such nice people. I don't know who could have done this to the Beavers who were so well liked by everyone. Then you think it must have been a person just walking by who just happened to pick that house, and you don't know what to do." The article continued the theme, stating that "Mount Pleasant is a community with a growing uneasiness, with undercurrents of fear and apprehension as it prepares to bury the murder victims this morning after funeral services at the St. Alphonsus Catholic church here."

The Thursday morning funeral was a closed-casket

service; the authorities recommended to the family that they not view Clementine's and Karol's bodies. The Gothic-style old brick church overflowed with flowers. An estimated 900 of the town residents attended the funeral, many of them Karol's fellow high school classmates. They filled the sanctuary, overflowed into the church basement, and scores more stood outside the church, beneath the soaring church steeple, where they could at least hear the service through a loudspeaker propped on a folding chair on the lawn.

Television news coverage showed Max being helped down the church stairs after the service, supported on both sides by his sons, nearly collapsing in grief. Among the pall bearers carrying Karol's coffin from the church were her close friend, Lance Poock, and her former boyfriend, Brad Gardner. The funeral procession drove across town from the church to the Saint Alphonsus Cemetery, on the southeast edge of McMillan Park. The procession passed by both Monte's and the Beavers' homes on its way. At the cemetery, on a treeless stretch of tombstones, Karol and her mother were buried alongside each other.

Meanwhile, the investigation into the murders continued. The police kept repeating requests for information from the public. They begged anyone who drove or walked by the Beavers' home late Sunday night or early Monday morning to contact the police. The police assured the public that they, together with the BCI and FBI, were working around the clock on the case.

A solicitation was taken up from the community and many people came forward to pledge money toward a $5,000 reward fund that would be paid out to anyone who came forward with information about the Beavers' murders that led to an arrest. Anyone with knowledge was encouraged to call the Mount Pleasant Police Department and ask for Chief Hagers or BCI Special Agent Larry Goepel. Notice of the reward ran repeatedly in the Mount Pleasant News. No one came forward; no one ever collected from the fund.

On December 21, 1978, Chief Hagers resigned as chief of police, but remained on the force as a Lieutenant Investigator. He explained to the City Council that he wanted to devote more time to the Beavers' murder investigation and couldn't do that while handling all the responsibilities of being Chief of Police. Before becoming police chief, Hagers had served as the police force's only full time investigator. That position had remained empty after his promotion to police chief. Hagers explained to the City Council that he believed the murders required a full-time investigator. The City Council accepted his resignation and appointed another officer as acting chief of police.

Although Investigator Hagers was able to devote renewed focus on the Beavers' murder investigation, he was unable to make any progress. No new clues were discovered, and what few leads law enforcement officers had to begin with led nowhere. As the weeks and months rolled by after the murders, the heavy presence of BCI agents in Mount Pleasant slowly faded away. The agents would return to Mount Pleasant soon enough, but only after another woman lost her life.

Meanwhile, the winter of 1978 to 1979 was one of the coldest on record in Mount Pleasant. On January 12, 1979, a historic blizzard hit the Midwest. It dropped almost two feet of snow in eastern Iowa. Among other things, the snow caved in the roof of one wing of rooms at the Iris Motel on the west side of Mount Pleasant. It was a long and dismal winter.

That winter, teacher Ms. Vincent noticed a change in Monte Seager at school. His mood and demeanor became gloomier, she thought, and he withdrew more from her and others. He didn't talk much in class and she found it increasingly difficult to persuade him to give a speech. His appearance changed, too, she noted. He let his hair grow out more and it seemed like he seldom combed it. He let it grow down over his eyes, almost like he was hiding in his hair. And overall, she thought, Monte appeared more unkempt.

But, at the time, Ms. Vincent made no connection between the changes she noticed in Monte and the murders of the Beavers. And because Monte had always been so quiet, so aloof from others, none of the students paid enough attention to him to notice any changes in him. If there were signs that Monte had anything to do with murdering and raping Karol, we students didn't see them.

1979 photo

Monte Seager in 1979 (photo from police file)

Soon, Monte's grades began to plummet even more. He was absent from school more and more. Then on April 12, 1979, Monte dropped out of high school.

The high school principal, Richard Van Tuyl, had been monitoring Monte's failing performance. He knew Monte had been kicked out of his father's home in December due to some family dispute, and that Monte was living with his aunt's family in a small house across the street behind the high school. The principal was also aware that Monte was shy and had no girlfriend and few friends. Principal Van Tuyl had worked with Monte's teachers in an attempt to intervene and assist him, but nothing had seemed to work.

But neither the principal, nor Monte's teachers, nor seemingly anyone else, thought there was any connection between Monte's downhill slide and the murders of his classmate and her mother back in October of 1978.

That is, not until the day after he dropped out of high school, April 13, 1979.

NINE

THE IRIS RESTAURANT

"There is no such thing as accident; it is fate misnamed."
— Napoleon Bonaparte

THE IRIS RESTAURANT WAS THE PREMIER DINING establishment in Mount Pleasant in the 1970s. It was owned and operated by Dave and Carmen Heaton, a warm and gregarious couple who, by the mid-1970s were in their mid-40s. The Heatons had owned the restaurant for many years. The Iris Restaurant was an upscale restaurant for Mount Pleasant, the type of place people sought out as the best venue to celebrate anniversaries, engagements, and birthdays. Awkward high school boys took their prom dates there.

The Iris Restaurant was located on Highway 34, on the west side of town, at the crest of a gentle hill. It sat not far from the Pizza Hut where teenagers hung out on

Friday and Saturday nights, and across the highway from the A&W restaurant. The Iris Restaurant was attached to the Iris Motel, an old one-story roadside motel with a couple dozen rooms, built back in the 1930s. In the late 1970s, the Iris Motel was a clean and well-maintained motel, the best one in Mount Pleasant.

The once fancy Iris Restaurant closed in the early 2000s and sat empty and abandoned, a dilapidated shell of its former self. In 2023, it was demolished. The adjacent motel, too, is now empty and forlorn. The tragic events that occurred there now erased from the earth.

The Iris Restaurant in 2022 (photo by author)

The Iris Restaurant in 2022 (photo by author)

When it was the popular restaurant that it was in the 1970s, patrons entered the Iris Restaurant on the west side of the building. They stepped into a long hallway. As one walked along the hallway, there were photos of the Iris Restaurant on the right wall; on the left was a wall of windows. At the end of the hall it opened up into a vestibule that served as a small waiting area. Stairs at the very end of the hall led to a banquet room on the second floor in the back of the restaurant, over the kitchen. In the banquet room, the restaurant would host rehearsal dinners and other private events. Indeed, the rehearsal dinner for my wedding would one day be held there. The kitchen was located to the left of the dining room as one entered the restaurant, past the waitress station, and in the back of the restaurant, reached by a short hallway. At the waitress station, waitresses would prepare salads and pour coffee, soda, and other non-alcoholic drinks. From there, waitresses and busboys would retrieve silverware, napkins, and condiments for the tables. Across from the waitress station was a door to a small room where employees clocked in and hung up their coats. In the back of that room was a small closet secured by a lock because liquor for and proceeds from the lounge were stored in there.

The Iris Restaurant entrance (photo from police file)

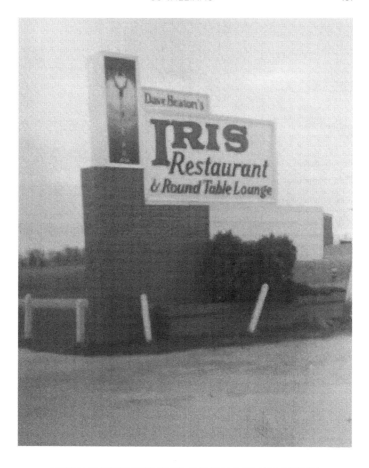

The Iris Restaurant sign (photo from police file)

When she worked there a few days a week, Carmen Heaton staffed the hostess station near the entry of the restaurant, next to the cash register. On Carmen's days off, Kay Young served as hostess. To the right was a small, low ceilinged, and dimly-lit carpeted lounge with a bar and a dozen tables with padded chairs. It was called the Round

Table Lounge. The dining area occupied the rest of the front of the building and was divided into several rooms.

The Roundtable Lounge (photo from police file)

Dave Heaton managed the restaurant, directing and supervising the kitchen and overseeing the staff. He was everywhere at once, it seemed. The Heatons were very nice people at a personal level, but they were demanding employers and expected the best from their employees. They pushed their employees hard and their standards were exacting. As a result, service was always excellent at the Iris Restaurant. Dave made sure a dining experience at the Iris was the best it could be. The restaurant had an excellent reputation and Dave was proud of the service he provided.

CJ WILLIAMS 133

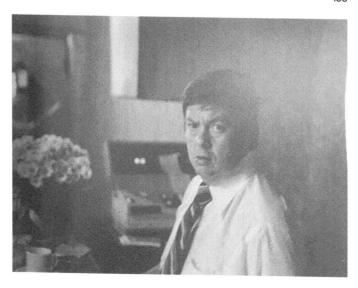

Dave Heaton (photo taken by Monte Seager, contained in police file)

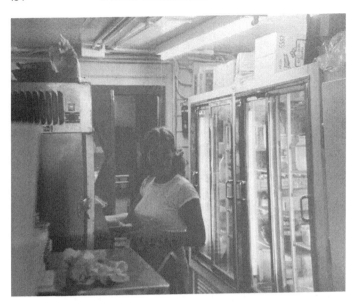

Former waitresses in the waitress station in former Iris Restaurant (photo taken by Monte Seager, contained in police file)

Former waitresses in the waitress station in former Iris Restaurant (photo taken by Monte Seager, contained in police file)

The back of the kitchen at the Iris Restaurant (photo from police file)

The Heatons had the dinner staff arrive for work at about four o'clock in the afternoon so they could be prepared for the dinner crowd by 5:00 p.m. When they arrived for work, whoever was working as the short order cook would fix all the staff a small meal before the shift started. The staff members all ate together at a table in the dining room. They ate quickly, and by 4:45 p.m. were on duty setting up for dinner. They then worked without a break until the restaurant stopped serving food at 9:00 p.m. By the time the restaurant staff finished cleaning up, they usually punched out of the restaurant around 10:00 p.m. The attached lounge stayed open until 1:00 a.m.

Each evening when the dinner crowd began to thin out, the Heatons would slowly close down the dining room by zones. They would make sure the staff had everything properly cleaned and set up for the next day, that everything was shut down and turned off in the kitchen, and that all the restaurant staff had clocked out. When, at last, the dining room was closed, Dave would clear the restaurant drawer of proceeds and take the receipts home with him. After the lounge closed in the early morning hours, the lounge staff would gather the proceeds from the lounge sales, place them in a bank bag, and lock them in the liquor closet for Dave to pick up the next day.

Monte Seager began working at the restaurant in the summer of 1978. Dave Heaton didn't know anything about Monte before hiring him. He knew of Monte's father, knew him to be blind, and knew him to frequent the seedy downtown bar. But Dave knew Harry only by sight. Harry wasn't the type to frequent Heaton's upscale lounge.

Dave was unaware that Monte had a criminal record. He didn't know Monte was on probation. This was back in a time when employers didn't routinely conduct criminal background checks on their employees. Had Dave known, he probably wouldn't have hired Monte. Dave was a demanding boss, but he was very protective of his staff and especially of his waitresses.

Monte started work at the restaurant as a dishwasher. But, a short time later, Dave needed to replace a short-order cook who had left, so he offered Monte the job. Monte accepted the promotion. Monte worked part-time, several nights a week and some weekends; around 28 hours a week. His duties were mostly to help the chef and occasionally serve as busboy.

Restaurant staff members remember Monte as generally being a nice guy, friendly, though not very talkative. Carmen Heaton thought Monte was a "nice kid." Especially when he first started, Monte was known to joke around a little with other employees. One former coworker remembers Monte swinging the large wooden paddle or spoon used to stir the jam as if it was a baseball bat, horsing around and smacking people in the butt with it. Beginning in the fall of 1978, Monte began bringing a camera to work from time to time and took a lot of photographs of the restaurant and its staff. No one was bothered by Monte taking photographs; he explained he was on the Target yearbook staff at school and was practicing his new hobby. Monte was a good photographer and shared copies of the photos he took with his coworkers.

Monte often asked other employees for rides home after work at the restaurant. It was a good two miles from the restaurant to his house and Monte didn't have a car. Someone on the staff almost always gave Monte a ride home, especially when the weather was poor. One waitress, though, never did. She couldn't articulate why when asked later, but she explained to me that she just didn't feel comfortable around him and always declined when he asked her for a ride.

After October 1978, this same waitress would later note Monte becoming more reserved. He would seldom talk with others. He seemed to have lost some weight and his acne, always a problem, became much worse. But, again, no one connected the change in Monte's behavior with the Beavers' murders.

As it happened, I also worked at the Iris Restaurant with Monte. I took a part-time job as a dishwasher there in February of 1979. Charlie Vestweber, my classmate and Monte's locker mate, helped me secure the job. Charlie was already working there as a dishwasher himself. Though Charlie quickly moved onto another job at a convenience store, I remained washing dishes at the Iris Restaurant until I quit in June to work at my father's store.

By the time I started working at the Iris Restaurant, Monte was already employed there. I didn't interact much with Monte at work. My dishwashing station was toward the back of the kitchen area, on the west wall, while Monte worked under the supervision of the chef toward the front of the kitchen, close to the waitress station, on the east side of the kitchen. Like the other employees, I would give Monte my order for the staff meal—invariably, he cooked me a hamburger—and I might visit with him a little during our staff meals before work. But Monte never spoke much to me, and I didn't say much to him. Monte didn't join in conversation often at these staff meals, and he sat a little away from others as we ate, in my recollection. Once in a while I would hear him talking with the chef and interacting with the wait staff about food orders, but it was all business with him. There was some of the usual lighthearted exchanges and joking among staff at work, but I don't recall Monte joining in much by the time I started working there. But then, again, I started working with Monte at the restaurant after Karol and Clementine had been murdered. If Monte had been a light-hearted employee before then, he certainly wasn't by the time I began working with him.

It was through my employment washing dishes at the Iris Restaurant that I also came to know a bartender there. Her name was Susan Wheelock. She went by Sue.

TEN
SUSAN WHEELOCK

"There are accidental parents, but there are no accidental children."

— Rick Warren

In 1946, Dr. Mark Wheelock was a handsome medical doctor, in his early 40s, temporarily working at the state hospital in Mount Pleasant. A pathologist by training, Dr. Wheelock specialized in cancer treatments. He had served in the Navy during World War II, in the Pacific Theatre, earning the rank of lieutenant commander. He was discharged from the Navy in 1946. His wife, Mary Louise, who went by "Mae," was originally from the Mount Pleasant area. They had a young daughter named Alice.

In December 1946, Mae took ill and was admitted to the medical hospital in Burlington, Iowa. She never left.

On April 11, 1947, Dr. Wheelock's 40-year-old wife tragically died at the hospital after a long illness. She was buried in the Forest Home Cemetery in Mount Pleasant.

In the early fall of 1947, about six months after his wife died, Dr. Wheelock and his daughter left Mount Pleasant. They moved to Chicago where Dr. Wheelock accepted a position as an associate professor and medical doctor at Northwestern University.

Frances Cathey was a young, local Mount Pleasant girl. She graduated from Mount Pleasant High School in 1944. Frances was an accomplished vocalist, often singing solos at local concerts. In 1948, she was 21 years old. Widower Dr. Wheelock married Frances on February 8, 1948, in Chicago. Together, they had a daughter, Susan Wheelock. Sue was more than a year old when her parents married.

Sue Wheelock, born out of wedlock, came into this world on January 12, 1947, in Mount Pleasant, while Dr. Wheelock was married to the first Mrs. Wheelock, while Mrs. Wheelock lay in a hospital bed. Sue was born less than four months before the first Mrs. Wheelock died.

Though Sue's parents eventually married, they never raised their illegitimate daughter. Instead, they passed on to Frances' parents, Thomas and Miriam Cathey, the responsibility of raising Sue. After Dr. Wheelock and Frances wed, they lived in Chicago but Sue remained in Mount Pleasant living in her grandparent's house, raised by her grandparents.

The social column of the local Mount Pleasant News reported from time to time occasions when one or both of

Sue's parents would come to Mount Pleasant to visit their daughter in the late 1940s and early 1950s. On one such occasion, while Sue's mother was in town visiting, the paper reported that six-year-old Sue had her hand crushed when her grandmother accidentally slammed a car door on Sue's hand. A couple years later, the social column reported that Sue's mother hosted a Halloween party for her daughter and 40 other children in a local hall. Typically, it was Sue's mother who came to visit, according to the newspaper accounts. Sue's father is reported in the social column visiting his daughter only once, in conjunction with a trip to Mount Pleasant to give a lecture at the state hospital. Dr. Wheelock's daughter Alice, from the doctor's prior marriage, visited her stepsister once as well, the local social column reported.

By late 1956, when Sue was about 10 years old, her mother divorced Dr. Wheelock. Sue's mother quickly remarried a man named Martin Frazer who lived in a small town near Mount Pleasant. Now known as Frances Frazer, Sue's mother had three more children with her new husband; two sons and a daughter. Sue, it appears, never lived with her mother and her mother's new husband. Rather, Sue remained estranged, continuing to be raised by her grandparents.

Sue attended school in Mount Pleasant, and graduated from its high school in May 1965.

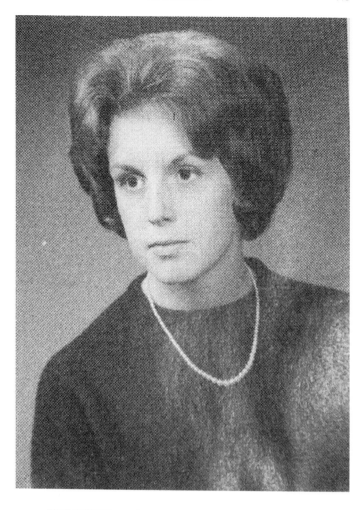

Sue Wheelock (photo by author of 1965 Mount Pleasant High School Yearbook)

A few months after Sue graduated from high school, on August 6, 1965, Sue's mother died at Mercy Hospital in Iowa City at the age of 39, after a long illness.

After graduating from Mount Pleasant High School, Sue moved to Topeka, Kansas to attend college for a short time before returning home again, without having earned a degree. Once back in Mount Pleasant, Sue worked in the Harlan Hotel restaurant for several years as a waitress. One of the other waitresses working there at the time was Kathy Beavers, one of Max and Clementine's older daughters. After working at the Harlan Hotel, Sue was employed for a period of time as a bookkeeper at a department store, but eventually started waitressing for Dave Heaton at the Iris Restaurant on the west side of town. By 1978, Sue had worked at the Iris Restaurant for several years. Sue and her cousin, Fran Worth, worked shifts as bartenders in the restaurant's lounge, working alternating nights.

In her free time, Sue sang and played the guitar, occasionally performing at weddings, taking after her birth mother in that way. Unmarried, and without children, Sue doted on her cats. Sue was also active in the community. Among other things, She served as President of the Henry County Planned Parenthood Board. But Sue had to earn a living, and so most evenings and nights found her waiting tables and bartending in the Round Table Lounge at the Iris Restaurant.

Sue went out on dates with men, just like most women her age. In 1977, she dated a pre-med student living in Iowa City. In the fall of 1978, about the time Karol and Clementine Beavers were murdered, Sue was dating a man named Allan Johnson who lived in a nearby town. By the spring of 1979, though, she had a new and somewhat serious boyfriend, Michael Moore. Sue told some of her friends that she and Michael had talked a little about marriage. Moore would initially tell officers later that he and Sue dated "loosely" and were more friends than lovers (though he conceded they had sex occasionally). In a later interview, though, Moore admitted that he and Sue had talked marriage, but they hadn't let many people know. He explained to the police that they were trying to keep it from Sue's grandmother because Sue didn't want to worry her grandmother who would end up being alone, her grandfather having died some years before.

By the late 1970s, Sue was in her early 30s. She was pretty with long auburn hair and a bright smile, considered tall for a woman at five feet, seven inches, and trim, weighing only 128 pounds. Sue was a very intelligent woman; "very intellectual," as Dave Heaton described her. But a friend also described Sue as kind of a hippie and a free spirit. Sue didn't drink alcohol, but she did have a history of using marijuana. Her boyfriend, Mike Moore, would later tell officers that Sue first smoked marijuana when she was in college in Kansas, and would smoke marijuana with him on occasion. Moore would mention to the police later that sometime in January 1978, Sue had obtained an ounce of marijuana from someone. But Sue wouldn't tell Moore where she got it.

Sue still lived at home with her grandmother in a modest two-story frame house located a couple blocks to the east of the high school on East Monroe Street, only a half-dozen blocks north of the Beavers' residence.

The Cathey home where Sue lived (photo by author)

Sue's friends and coworkers described Sue as a "super nice person" and kind to everyone. She was notably kind to Monte Seager, some of her coworkers would later recall. She gave Monte a ride home on a couple occasions. Monte once asked Sue for a ride to Iowa City. Sue later explained to her boyfriend, Mike Moore, that she politely turned Monte down, telling him that she didn't go out with young kids.

Though extremely nice to and pleasant with others, Sue was not a light-hearted person. The Heatons would later contrast her to the happy-go-lucky attitude of the rest of the waitresses who worked for them. They noted that Sue seemed to carry some heavy weight on her shoulders. Sue didn't share details of her childhood with the Heatons or her friends, not even her boyfriend. Nevertheless, they knew enough from what little she did reveal to understand that Sue had a troubled childhood. One of Sue's friends describe Sue's demeanor as usually fairly serious, as if there was a cloud over her. It was also rumored that she had been raped in the past, perhaps during the brief time she lived in Topeka.

The cloud that hung over Sue descended upon her on April 13, 1979.

ELEVEN
MURDER AT THE IRIS

"Nobody owns life, but anyone who can pick up a frying pan owns death."
— William S. Burroughs

IN APRIL 1979, FRIDAY THE 13TH WAS GOOD FRIDAY. Late that evening, there was a full moon. It was a chilly night; the temperature had only risen to 58 degrees that afternoon and after the sun went down it dipped down to just a little bit above freezing.

In many ways, it was a typical night at the Iris Restaurant. The usual patrons came at the usual times. The restaurant itself was particularly busy this night, but the lounge was a little slow. One waitress failed to show up, so only three of them were handling all four zones in the restaurant. Sue Wheelock, then 32 years old, was manning the Round Table Lounge that night. She didn't usually work on Friday nights, but this particular night she was substituting for the regular Friday night bartender, her cousin Fran Worth. Sue had traded nights with Fran because Sue planned to go to Iowa City on Saturday night with her boyfriend, Mike Moore, to attend the ballet. Neither Monte nor I happened to be working that Good Friday night.

But Monte showed up at the restaurant that evening, around 7:00 p.m., anyway. He slipped into the kitchen through the back door, trying to avoid being seen by Dave Heaton. Once inside, Monte asked several of his coworkers if he could borrow $20. They all turned him down and, after a few minutes of pleading, Monte left without having been seen by Dave and without the $20 he was after.

Around 9:00 p.m., Monte entered the Casey's General Store, a convenience store on Highway 34, about a mile east of the Iris Restaurant. Charlie Vestweber happened to be manning the front counter that evening. Charlie noticed that Monte had been drinking. Monte's eyes were bloodshot and his speech impaired. Monte was with his friend, Bill Snyder, and a female whom Charlie did not know. They had driven up in Snyder's car. Monte bought a pack of Marlboro cigarettes and the group left after the female used the restroom. Charlie didn't notice which way they went when Snyder drove out of the parking lot.

The Iris Restaurant closed down as usual around 10:00 p.m., and the kitchen staff clocked out close to 10:30 p.m. after finishing the final cleaning of their work areas. The Round Table Lounge stayed open until 1:00 a.m. as usual, serving drinks to some of the regulars. Mike Moore, Sue's boyfriend, spent some time in the lounge that evening, eating a steak sandwich and drinking a couple beers, chatting with Sue when she wasn't busy. A couple patrons remember the couple talking amicably and laughing occasionally. Mike left around midnight and went home. He later recalled that Sue was in a good mood and seemed happy.

Dave Heaton checked in with Sue near midnight. She told him she planned on closing a little early because it was so slow, and Dave approved. Dave then left and went home, taking the restaurant proceeds with him, as usual. A little before 1:00 a.m., the last couple customers left the lounge and Sue began closing it down. A waitress from the restaurant who was good friends with Sue had stuck around for a little while. She talked with Sue for a few minutes as Sue began the closing down process, cleaning up the last few glasses. But the waitress soon announced that she had to go home because she had to get up early the next morning to work the breakfast shift, starting at 6:30 a.m. She said goodbye to Sue and left the bar a little after 1:00 a.m.

After her friend left, Sue followed her usual closing routine. After she cleaned up, she opened the register and put all the cash in a moneybag, and began tallying up the receipts. She needed to leave $131.00 in small bills and rolls of coins in the safe for the next day; the rest of the proceeds she would put in the moneybag and then lock it up in the closet in the back of the employee's coat room. Sue tallied up the bills and cash register receipts on a slip of paper, next to the register. Sue must have heard something back in the kitchen, however, because she left her tallying midway when she went to investigate the sound.

When Sue reached the back of the kitchen, she suddenly came upon an intruder. She surprised the intruder at the entrance to the kitchen, just as she was surprised by him. The man had been hiding upstairs in the banquet room while the restaurant and bar were being closed down for the night. When he thought everyone had left the restaurant, he came down the back stairs and into the kitchen. But he was wrong. Sue was still there, and caught him.

Back of the Iris Restaurant Kitchen (photo from police file)

The man immediately attacked Sue. She turned to run, but he was close on her heels and chased her a short distance, catching up with her near the waitress station. At some point, the man had grabbed the large wooden paddle Dave Heaton used in the kitchen to stir his strawberry preserves in a big vat. The paddle was made of hard cherry wood, and was about a yard long and one inch thick, being slightly wider at one end. The man repeatedly struck Sue in the head with the paddle so hard it broke off splinters from the wider paddle part of the stick. Sue stumbled and fell to the tile floor when she reached the waitress station. Before she could rise again and attempt to flee, the man dropped the broken paddle and grabbed the closest objects within reach to use as weapons—two-liter glass soda bottles. The man continued to beat Sue savagely and repeatedly in the head with the bottles, smashing several of the bottles over her head. The man kept beating Sue with the bottles over and over again until she crumpled to the floor face first, unconscious and bloody.

Satisfied that Sue would never rise again, the man stopped beating her and dropped the last bottle he was using from his hand. Then he slipped into the lounge and began rummaging around looking for loot. He found the bar proceeds Sue was counting (about $300 or $400 in cash, some checks) and pocketed the money. He also found Sue's purse and took it and whatever cash she had inside. Then he fled the restaurant into the dark night.

Early the following morning, before the sun rose, Dave Heaton drove to the restaurant to open it up for Saturday's breakfast crowd. Dave was often the breakfast cook there on weekends and was known for his sumptuous breakfasts, especially his homemade strawberry preserves. He arrived a little after 6:00 a.m. When he pulled his car into the driveway, Dave immediately noticed some things were amiss. Sue's Mercury Cougar was still parked outside the restaurant. That seemed odd to Dave. Sue would have driven it home, normally; she didn't leave her car parked in the restaurant lot. Dave also noticed that the outdoor lights were still on, as were the lights in the lounge area. Sue was usually very good about shutting off all the lights before she left at night.

Dave parked his car, got out, and walked up to the main entrance of the restaurant and tested the door. It was still locked. He took out his key and entered the restaurant. He walked down the hallway, past the hostess station on his way to the kitchen. Inside the restaurant, the lights normally left on overnight, one over the fireplace in the main dining room and one over the waitress station, provided dim illumination to the still dark interior of the restaurant.

As Dave passed the hostess station, he turned left to head into the kitchen, but stopped abruptly at the entry to the waitress station. There, at his feet, Dave was shocked to see Sue's bloody body. She was lying face down on the tile floor near the waitress station, her arms down along her sides, shattered glass all around her. Blood had pooled beneath her, especially near her head. Blood spatters speckled the walls, equipment, and pots and pans in the narrow walkway. The back of Sue's head was a bloody mess with pieces of glass embedded in her long hair. Dave quickly knelt down next to Sue, calling out her name several times. When he cautiously touched her leg, she moaned weakly in response, but didn't speak.

Heaton jumped up and ran to the phone at the hostess station, near the front of the restaurant, urgently calling for an ambulance.

"Get here fast!" Dave yelled into the phone, "Someone is laying on the floor and it's bad!"

As soon as he hung up with the ambulance service, Dave called the police, urging them to come quick.

Then Dave stepped outside the restaurant and stood near the front door, waiting for help to arrive. Dave was scared and felt helpless. As he stood there waiting, Dave didn't know whether the attacker or attackers were still in the building, and didn't know if he was also in danger. He knew Sue was still alive and desperately needed medical assistance, but was aware there was nothing he could do to help her.

The police and ambulance crew arrived quickly, but the minutes it took for them to arrive seemed like hours for Dave.

Mount Pleasant Police Officers Joe Baxter and Bob Griffith, the only two officers on duty, were the first to arrive at the scene. As they pulled up to the restaurant in separate squad cars, they saw Dave Heaton outside waving his hands in an excited manner, urging the officers to hurry. Dave ran up to the officers as they were getting out of their squad cars. In a rush of words, he told them that his bartender, Sue, was lying on the floor. Not comprehending the full gravity of what happened, Officer Baxter asked Dave if she had a heart attack or something. "No," Dave replied. He explained to the officers that she had been violently attacked and she was lying in a pool of blood. He told the officers that she was still alive and they needed to hurry.

Dave led the officers inside and to the waitress station where Sue was lying face down, arms to her side, palms up. Officer Baxter observed sharp pieces of glass protruding from the back of her head. He knelt down next to her and felt for a pulse on Sue's neck. He could detect a pulse, but it was weak, and her breathing was shallow. Officer Baxter told Officer Griffith to get on the radio to the ambulance and tell them to "get a move on it" because she was still alive. He also instructed Griffith to call in Investigator Hagers, the chief of police, and the sheriff. Because the Iris was just outside the city limits, the crime scene was technically the primary jurisdiction of the sheriff's office. Concerned that the attacker may still be in the restaurant, Officers Baxter and Griffith quickly searched the building, but they didn't find anyone else present.

While the officers were searching the restaurant, Investigator Hagers arrived. He found Dave inside the restaurant and saw Sue face down in a pool of blood. Investigator Hagers knew Sue personally; he was a frequent patron at the Iris Restaurant and the Round Table Lounge. Hagers could tell that Sue was still alive, but he could see she was severely injured and in need of emergency medical aid.

Investigator Hagers found a long, splintered piece of wood near Sue's body. He picked it up and showed it to

Dave Heaton who immediately recognized that it was part of the paddle he used for stirring his strawberry preserves. The rest of the paddle was missing. The paddle was always kept in the back of the restaurant, near the large vat used for making the jam, Dave told Hagers.

The ambulance personnel arrived almost immediately after Hagers. They also found Sue still alive. She was breathing rapidly now. They cleared some of the glass away, turned her over, and placed her on a backboard. Then they rushed her out to the waiting ambulance and sped to the emergency room at the local hospital, less than a mile away. There, emergency room doctors immediately assessed the seriousness of Sue's injuries. They could tell from her vital signs and the extent of her head injuries that she was beyond any help they could render in the local, small town hospital. Within an hour, Sue was transferred by life-flight helicopter to the University of Iowa Hospital in Iowa City.

Before long, Sheriff Richard Droz and several of his deputies arrived at the restaurant and took over primary responsibility for the investigation. They and other law enforcement officers scoured the restaurant and the surrounding area, including the attached motel, looking for clues. There was no sign of forced entry into the restaurant. In the upstairs banquet room, officers found signs that someone had been hiding up there. A trail of blood ran from the back of the kitchen, where the attacker must have first encountered Sue, up to the waitress station where Dave had found Sue on the floor. In the middle of the trail were clear shoe impressions with a herringbone pattern.

In the blood around Sue's body, officers found additional impressions from the soles of shoes. Some appeared to have the same herringbone pattern seen in the blood trail from the back of the kitchen. But with Dave Heaton, the police, and all the rescue personnel having stepped all over the area, it was difficult to distinguish one shoeprint from another. The focus had been on trying to save Sue's life, not preserving shoe impressions in her blood. As part of the investigation officers obtained shoe impressions from everyone who set foot in the kitchen that day.

It was apparent to the officers that whoever beat Sue to a bloody pulp had been inside the restaurant when she was closing down the lounge. The officers concluded that robbery was the obvious motive; cash had been taken from the now-empty money bag on the bar counter where Sue had been calculating the night's proceeds.

Officers canvassed the area, interviewing people working and staying in the motel. No one had seen or heard anything suspicious, though. The officers noted that large blowers operating to cool the freezer and refrigeration equipment in the kitchen made a fairly loud noise in the area between the restaurant and the motel where people were staying. That would have made it difficult for anyone outside the restaurant to hear what was happening in the kitchen area. Additionally, the wing of the motel closest to the restaurant was still unoccupied because workers were not yet finished with repairs from the roof collapse in January, due to the heavy winter snows.

Later that morning, however, the owner of the Iris Motel told the police still at the scene that he discovered someone had broken into Room 26. When officers investigated the break-in into room 26, they found shoe impressions with the same herringbone pattern left on the ground outside the window where the intruder had broken into the room. On one of the impressions, the number "10" was clearly visible. The officers traced the footprints from the back window of Room 26 to the back of the Iris Restaurant, and then back to the window again. It was clear the person who left the prints had entered the restaurant through an unlocked back window in the back of the kitchen area. It wasn't clear why the attacker had broken into Room 26; nothing appeared to be missing. Left in the room, on the bed, was a cassette tape player with a tape of "Toys in the Attic" by the rock group Aerosmith. Also on the bed was a pack of Marlboro cigarettes.

Room 26 at the Iris Motel (photo by author)

Meanwhile, medical specialists at the University of Iowa Hospital struggled to save Sue Wheelock's life. By the time she arrived at the hospital by helicopter, Sue had no blood pressure. She had deep lacerations above her right eye and many more on the top of her head, but the most severe damage was to the left side of her skull. The severe beating had ripped a large portion of her scalp away from her skull there, and her skull was fractured. The fracture was nearly seven inches long. Sue had suffered internal hemorrhaging in her brain beneath the fracture.

All of her significant injuries were isolated to her head. The doctors found no sign the attacker sexually assaulted Sue, though they did find she had a large bruise in her pelvic region. The pathologist later determined that the bruise may have been inflicted during the assault.

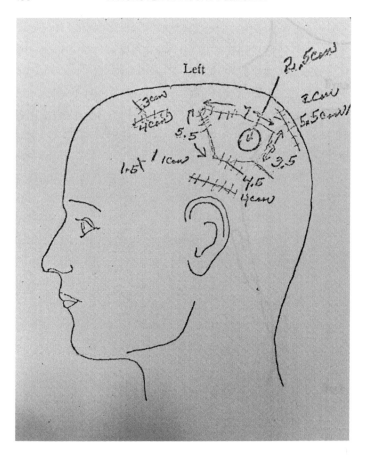

Autopsy drawing of Susan Wheelock's head (photo from police file)

Despite the valiant efforts by medical staff to save Sue's life, it was not enough. About 5:00 p.m. on April 17, 1979, three days after she was severely beaten, Sue died from her injuries. She never regained consciousness.

It didn't surprise Sue's friends, given how kind Sue was, to learn that she was an organ donor. Doctors harvested her eyes, kidneys, and other organs. Sue gave new sight and life to six other people through her generosity.

Susan Wheelock's funeral took place on Saturday, April 21 (the day before what would have been Karol Beavers' 17th birthday). It was a sunny and mild spring day. The ceremony took place at the Iowa Wesleyan Chapel. Sue's father, Dr. Mark Wheelock, and the grandmother who raised her, survived Sue and attended her funeral. So did Sue's stepsiblings from her mother's second marriage.

Sue was buried in the Forest Home Cemetery, just across the street from the Catholic cemetery where Clementine and Karol lay in peace. The graves, those of the Beavers and Wheelock, were less than 100 yards apart. No one knew at the time that they were the victims of the same murderer.

TWELVE
MONTE CHARGED

"Injustice is relatively easy to bear; what stings is justice." –
H. L. Mencken

BECAUSE OFFICERS COULDN'T FIND EVIDENCE OF forced entry at the restaurant, suspicion immediately turned to those who worked there. Officers generated a list of current and former employees from Dave Heaton. Then, over the course of the next few days, officers fingerprinted all of the employees. But because officers concluded it was an inside job, they recognized that latent fingerprints would be of little help; employees would naturally have left prints in the restaurant. Indeed, the officers recovered my latent prints in the restaurant near my work station. Where they didn't find latent prints was on any of the remains of the glass bottles the assailant used to beat Sue to death, or the door knobs or other objects where the attacker was apparently hiding in the upstairs room before the attack. Nor were any latent prints apparently recovered from Room 26, the room it appeared the attacker had broken into either before or after the attack.

On Easter Sunday following Sue's beating, law enforcement officers at the Henry County Law Center interviewed many of the employees of the Iris Restaurant, including me. And Monte Seager. They asked all of us what we knew about Sue, whether she had any enemies, and who we thought might have attacked her. They also questioned us about where we were the night of the attack, when we last worked at the restaurant, and what we knew about the restaurant operations, particularly the procedures for closing the restaurant and lounge at the end of the night and the handling of the day's proceeds. They asked us about our coworkers and whether we had any suspicion that one of them was involved in the burglary and attack on Sue Wheelock. The officers also asked what shoes we normally wore, and they examined the bottoms of our shoes, even temporarily taking custody of many of our tennis shoes for comparison purposes. My shoes didn't match the herringbone shoe impressions left at the crime scene.

My interview lasted only about a half-hour. I was of no help. I wasn't working the night of the attack. I hadn't seen anything unusual the night before when I did work. I didn't really know Sue well, and had no idea who would have committed the crime. I knew nothing about the closing procedures or the handling of money. When they asked me about other coworkers, I told them whom I worked with most often. I told them I couldn't think of any of my coworkers doing something like this. They asked me specifically about Monte Seager. I told them I didn't know of any contact between Monte and Sue. I told them I thought Monte was a good kid.

Other witnesses were more helpful than I was. Several witnesses placed Monte at the restaurant that night, and on previous occasions when he wasn't supposed to be there. Officers also learned from some of these witnesses that Monte had broken into the restaurant in the past. Several of Monte's friends told officers that on several occasions when they were hanging out with Monte, he would have them drive to the restaurant after hours, after the restaurant had closed. They told the officers that Monte would jump out of the car, go back behind the restaurant, be gone a few minutes, and then return with alcohol and sometimes food. These friends told officers they believed Monte snuck in through a back window. When shown photographs of the cassette tape player officers found in Room 26, a couple of Monte's associates also thought they recognized it and said it belonged to Monte.

Dave Heaton recalled that on April 9, just a few days before Sue was attacked, he was sitting at the bar in the lounge near midnight when he caught the glimpse of someone walking into the kitchen, which had been closed down for hours. Dave impetuously followed the unknown person to investigate. When Dave reached the kitchen, he found Monte there. Dave confronted Monte about what he was doing in the kitchen after hours. Monte claimed he was there to retrieve some cigarettes he had left behind.

Dave ordered Monte out of the building, and followed Monte out the front door to make sure he left.

Bill Snyder was another coworker at the Iris Restaurant whom officers questioned. Snyder and Monte were also friends. Snyder told officers that he was with Monte on the evening of April 13th, driving around town in Snyder's car. Snyder told officers that Monte was trying to buy marijuana from people. Snyder told the officers that Monte and he spoke with several people, trying to find someone who would sell them marijuana. Snyder explained, however, that they couldn't find any marijuana available. One friend of theirs let Monte take a few drags on a marijuana cigarette, but that was the closest they came to finding marijuana.

At some point that evening, Snyder told the officers Monte directed Snyder to drive to the Iris Restaurant. While Snyder waited outside in his car, Monte went inside the restaurant through the back door. Once inside, he tried to borrow money from some of the employees. When no one would loan him money, Monte eventually gave up and left, rejoining Snyder in his car.

Snyder said that for a while that evening a female friend, Mary Lou Wellington, rode around with Monte and him. Snyder acknowledged that the three of them had stopped into the Casey's convenience store (consistent with Charlie Vestweber's observation). But Snyder said Wellington rode around with them for only a short time. Snyder said she wasn't with them when, earlier in the evening, he had dropped Monte off at the restaurant in his failed effort to borrow money from one of the employees.

Snyder explained to the officers that after dropping off Wellington back at her house, he and Monte continued to drive around town for a couple more hours. Eventually, somewhere around midnight, Snyder said that Monte had Snyder drop him off again near the Iris Motel. Snyder then went home, he told the officers. Snyder said he didn't have any more contact with Monte after that.

Like other Iris Restaurant employees, Monte also came to the law center voluntarily that Easter Sunday, at an officer's request. He wasn't in formal police custody at the time. Monte arrived at the police department about 6:30 that Sunday night. The officers' questioning of him focused on the events at the Iris Restaurant.

Monte told the officers that on the night of April 13, he was cruising around Mount Pleasant with Bill Snyder in Snyder's Chevrolet Monte Carlo. Monte said he had been smoking weed and drinking whiskey earlier that evening. He told the officers that he and Snyder were trying to buy more marijuana. Monte admitted going to the Iris Restaurant earlier in the evening and asking some of his coworkers for money, but said they all turned him down. He told the police that he and Snyder picked up Monte's cousin, Mary Lou Wellington. He said the three of them drove around Mount Pleasant looking to buy marijuana, but were unsuccessful and eventually he went home.

Monte explained to the officers that he had been living with his aunt and uncle Wellington the last few months. Monte's aunt, his father Harry's sister, had married a cousin of Walter Wellington many years ago. The Wellingtons lived in a small house across the street from the back side of the high school and, as it happened, only a couple blocks from where Sue Wheelock lived with her grandmother. Harry had kicked Monte out of his house back in December after Monte put his foot through the ceiling while climbing around in the attic to retrieve Christmas decorations.

When asked what he was wearing that night, Monte told the officers that the clothes he was wearing in the interview were the same clothes he wore on the night of April 13. Officers asked Monte if they could look at his shoes. He obliged. Monte was wearing Adidas athletic shoes. Turning the shoes over, the officers observed they had a herringbone pattern on the sole, the same pattern that matched the pattern made in Sue's blood on the floor of the restaurant, the same pattern made in the dirt outside the back of Room 26. This included the size 10 notation on the sole.

After listening to Monte's story for a while, the officers confronted Monte about finding a cassette tape player and cigarettes in Room 26, and told him that other witnesses had said the cassette player belonged to him. They showed Monte a photograph of the cigarettes and tape player. They also told him that the soles of his shoes matched the pattern of the footprints found outside the window of Room 26. Confronted with this evidence, Monte grudgingly confessed that he broke into Room 26 of the Iris Motel, and that the cassette player and cigarettes were his.

Monte said that after everyone at the Iris Restaurant refused to loan him money, he walked out of the restaurant through the kitchen's back door and proceeded to walk down behind the row of motel rooms. These rooms were unoccupied because workers were still repairing the roof damage from the massive snowfall that winter. At one point he said he came across a stick laying on the ground and used it to smash out the rear window of one of the rooms—Room 26. He said he broke into the room to steal a television or radio, but didn't take anything at that point and left. He claimed he acted alone.

Monte told the officers he walked out the front door of the motel room and met back up with Snyder. The officers noted that this was inconsistent with Snyder's version of events, which had Monte walking out of the back of the restaurant to rejoin him after Monte's unsuccessful attempt to borrow money. By Snyder's description of where he was parked while waiting for Monte, he would have seen Monte walk behind the row of motel rooms, but did not mention ever seeing Monte do so. Snyder's version was also inconsistent with Monte approaching Snyder's car from the front of the motel.

Monte continued to claim that, after he was unsuccessful borrowing money, he and Snyder and, later, two others, drove around Mount Pleasant looking to buy marijuana. He again said they were unsuccessful in finding anyone who would sell them weed. After they drove around some more, Monte said he had Snyder drop him back off near the Iris Motel. Monte told the officers he re-entered Room 26 through the back window and stayed there for about a half hour—between 12:30 a.m. and 1:00 a.m. Monte claimed he went back to the motel room with the same intent of stealing the television, but ended up not taking it because he decided it was too heavy to carry home. Monte claimed he left the motel room out the front door around 1:00 a.m. and walked to the Wellington home, a couple miles away, and went to bed in his room. He denied ever re-entering the Iris Restaurant.

The officers kept asking Monte about re-entering the restaurant after hours, but Monte vehemently denied having anything to do with beating Sue Wheelock, or having burglarized the restaurant. He admitted only to breaking into Room 26.

While questioning Monte, the officers had noticed Monte had several fresh wounds on his hands. They also noticed there were stains on Monte's pants that the officers thought were possibly blood spatters. After about two and a half hours of questioning, the officers let Monte leave.

After interrogating Monte, the officers knew he had broken into Room 26, and were fairly certain he was involved in beating Sue Wheelock and burglarizing the restaurant. But they didn't have quite enough yet to charge him. They needed more evidence before they could charge him with assaulting Sue.

There was also some suspicion among the officers and others that Monte didn't act alone that night. The officers had observed a second set of footprints outside Room 26 that had not yet been identified, and never would be. There were also possibly some unknown footprints in the restaurant itself, but the markings were not distinctive enough to allow easy comparison, especially after all the foot traffic in the kitchen and around Sue's body as rescue personnel attempted to save her.

It also seemed odd that one killer would use two different weapons—a paddle and glass bottles—to kill the victim. The weapons were located in two different parts of the kitchen, far apart from each other. The paddle was always kept in the far back corner of the kitchen, near the vat Heaton used to make his strawberry preserves. The glass soda bottles were toward the very front of the kitchen, in the waitress's station. How a single attacker came to use weapons from two different areas was hard to explain. Why a single attacker would choose to use two different weapons wasn't all that clear either. Indeed, the use of two different weapons from two different places in the kitchen suggested two attackers were at work.

Investigator Hagers and Dave Heaton remained skeptical that Monte had acted alone in burglarizing the restaurant and beating Sue to death. In particular, they suspected that Monte's friend, Dennis Cornell, was involved. They knew Monte hung out a lot with Cornell. Dave had seen Cornell at the restaurant before, on other evenings, talking with Monte. Dave always had an uneasy feeling about Cornell. And Hagers knew Cornell had been in trouble with the law before.

Other witnesses also speculated that Dennis Cornell was involved in the burglary and attack on Wheelock. Eventually, police officers tracked Cornell down and questioned him at length about whether he was involved in the break-in and attack. He denied it. Cornell offered several conflicting explanations about where he was, what he was doing that night, and what he knew about the break-in and beating. His story changed a couple times, claiming at first he was at one place with certain friends, then claiming he was at another place with other friends. Officers followed up with those friends, all of whom were unable to verify either version of Cornell's story. Although Cornell's story didn't check out, there was also nothing solid placing him at the restaurant that night. One witness did claim to have seen fresh scratches or injuries on Cornell's face the night after the attack, but officers didn't see any such marks on Cornell when they interviewed him just a couple days later. Also, Cornell's shoes didn't have a herringbone pattern. They found no property belonging to Cornell at the scene, like they did with Monte. There was just no real evidence that Cornell was involved in the attack. It was pure speculation.

So, the police focused their investigation exclusively on Monte. On Monday, April 16, 1979, police officers and sheriff's deputies obtained a search warrant for the home Monte had shared with his father, Harry, and Monte's stepmother, Sharon Gaylord. The officers executed the warrant at 2:30 a.m., an unusual time for officers to execute a search warrant. Typically, law enforcement officers execute search warrants during normal waking hours and reserve night-time searches for instances when there's some urgency, like fear that evidence will be destroyed, or concerns about officers' safety while executing the warrant. The affidavit in support of the search warrant didn't relate any such fears and doesn't help explain why officers chose to execute the search warrant in the middle of the night.

Whatever the reason for the timing, about 2:30 a.m. officers were knocking on the front door of the Seager home. The search team included officers from the sheriff's department and the police department, including the Henry County Sheriff, Richard Droz, and Investigator Hagers. Harry Seager opened the door in response to officers' insistent knocking. When Investigator Hagers announced who they were and why they were there, Harry's only response was: "What did he do, now?"

Monte wasn't living at his father's residence at the time of the search warrant; he was still living at his Aunt Wellington's house. So, Monte was not there. Harry's common law wife, Sharon, was home. Donnie, Monte's little brother, was also staying there, on break from the group home he was living at in Burlington. Based on what the officers seized from the house it was possible that Monte had recently been spending some time there, or else Donnie had obtained some items from Monte.

The search warrant authorized officers to search and seize evidence related to the break-in at the Iris Motel, the attack on Sue Wheelock, and the burglary of the restaurant. Among items officers found and seized in Monte's room was a photograph of Sue Wheelock. They also seized more of Monte's shoes, a pair of blue jeans and some shirts, two $20 bills, and a plastic bag with some marijuana. Officers also recovered six rolls of coins (two rolls each of quarters, dimes, and nickels), quantities and denominations that could be consistent with what the Iris Restaurant kept on hand to start the next day's till. These could have been the coins Sue had set aside during her final, incomplete tallying of the register the night she was attacked. They could have been coins stolen during the burglary.

Unrelated to the Wheelock murder, officers also observed several wallets belonging to high school students in Monte's room. There was no money in any of the wallets, but the students' identification cards and other identifying information remained. Additionally, officers found a small, empty box for matches, inside of which was the torn part of a matchbook from the Iris Restaurant on which someone had written: "The rifles [*sic*] true caliber is magnum 22."

During the search, officers also happened to observe a disassembled .22 caliber Mossberg rifle in a suitcase that also contained some of Monte's clothes. Both Monte's father and stepmother told the officers that the weapon belonged to Monte. Officers also observed a plastic box containing CCI .22 caliber ammunition. The officers didn't seize the weapon or ammunition, though, because it wasn't evidence related to the Wheelock murder and the search warrant didn't authorize officers to seize these items. But it wasn't lost on the officers that the Beavers were killed with CCI .22 caliber ammunition.

During the search officers interviewed Monte's father and stepmother about Monte's whereabouts on the night Sue Wheelock was attacked. Neither Harry nor Sharon had much information to offer. They simply didn't know where Monte was that night. He was living at his aunt's house at the time and they explained to the officers they had no knowledge of his movements the night Sue was attacked.

Officers also expanded the scope of questioning of Monte's parents beyond the attack on Sue Wheelock to include what they knew about Monte's possible involvement in the Beavers' murders. Monte's father and stepmother both opined that Monte seemed normal in the days following the Beavers' murders. He had never mentioned Karol, his stepmother recalled, other than to say he attended school with her. Sharon told officers that Monte told her how he learned about the murders. Monte told Sharon that when he arrived at school the morning after the murders he observed girls crying outside the school, but said he didn't know why until he heard other students talking about the murders. In short, neither Harry nor Sharon offered any information to officers that was helpful on the Beavers' murders.

The officers concluded the search of the Seager home around 3:47 a.m. The search warrant also authorized seizing clothing and other evidence, such as hair and blood samples, from Monte himself. So, at 3:56 a.m., officers arrived at the Wellington home where Monte had been staying with his aunt and uncle. The officers seized the clothes Monte had been wearing during their questioning of him the day before, including his shoes with the herringbone pattern on the soles. The officers then took Monte to the police station where they executed the warrant on Monte by taking the blood and hair samples. When they finished, they drove Monte back to his aunt and uncle's house and released him. Laboratory tests would ultimately show that the stains on Monte's pants were indeed blood stains, and they matched Sue Wheelock's blood type. And a forensic examiner would opine that Monte's shoes matched the impressions left at the crime scene.

Later on the same Monday when officers searched Monte's house, they also searched Monte's locker at the high school. The way the officers executed the search warrant was unusual. The officers went to the principal's office and spoke to the principal to learn who Monte shared a locker with. Then the officers had the school administration call Charlie Vestweber to the office. When Charlie arrived at the principal's office, the officers asked Charlie to go through the locker he shared with Monte and to bring all of Monte's belongings to the officers waiting in the administration office.

Charlie did as he was told. Monte had not left much in the locker; just a spiral notebook, some loose school papers, and a few books. It turns out that Charlie had already searched through Monte's belongings on his own, after Monte had quit school the week before and word quickly got out that Monte was a possible suspect in the attack on Sue Wheelock. Charlie had already thumbed through Monte's notebook. Initially, Charlie had not seen anything of particular interest in Monte's notebooks and papers. Charlie did notice, however, some impressions made on a sheet of paper in the notebook where Monte had written something on the preceding page then ripped that page out of the notebook. Being a clever guy Charlie had taken a blank sheet of paper, placed it over the top sheet of paper in Monte's notebook, and used the edge of a pencil to lightly raise the impressions from the paper beneath.

Using this technique, Charlie recalled that he could make out some of what Monte had written on the missing page. Charlie recalled that Monte had written something about selling his soul to the devil in exchange for which Monte could get any woman he wanted. Charlie recalled the writing also said something along the lines that if the girls don't do what Monte wanted, the contract would be broken. Charlie didn't see any specific references to Karol. Charlie had thrown away the paper he used to raise the impressions.

When Charlie handed over the notebook and Monte's other belongings to the officers, however, he told the officers about his previous discovery from the impressions left on the paper. Charlie assumed officers would later use the same technique he used to find the same impressions. If they did, it was never reported. The police reports about the search of the items from Monte's locker mention Charlie telling them about the writings he discovered in Monte's notebook, but the reports don't relate that officers ever raised impressions of the writings Charlie recalled. The spiral notebooks were still in police evidence when, years later, I went through them while researching this book. Though curious, it wouldn't have been appropriate for me to manipulate the evidence in police custody, so I never tried myself to see if the wording Charlie saw was still visible by raising the impressions.

Two days after the searches, on Wednesday, April 18,

1979, officers arrested Monte for the attack on Sue Whee-lock and the burglary of the Iris Restaurant. Sue had died the day before. Officers arrested Monte at his aunt's house without incident. The authorities charged Monte with first degree murder, robbery in the first degree, burglary in the first degree, and theft in the first degree. Later that day, the judge set Monte's bond at $130,000.

Several days after Monte's arrest, his stepmother, Sharon Gaylord, came to the law enforcement center and asked to speak to Investigator Hagers. He met her in the lobby. She was crying and upset. She explained to Hagers that she couldn't live with the weight of it any longer and had to tell him the truth. Hagers invited her into his office and asked her to sit down and tell him what was on her mind. Gaylord started by saying that she hadn't told the officers everything when they questioned her about Monte's behavior after the Beavers' murders. Hagers encouraged her to tell him what she knew.

Sharon told Hagers that the day after the Beavers' murders, Monte came home early from school claiming he was sick. She recalled leaving a little bit later to go grocery shopping. When she returned home, she saw Monte burning something that looked like clothes in a burn barrel located behind their house. It was normal for the Seagers to burn trash in the burn barrel, she explained; indeed, it was supposed to be one of Monte's chores, along with washing dishes. But Monte wasn't good at doing chores and often left the trash pile up a long time before burning it. So his sudden act of burning trash, especially when he was allegedly sick, seemed unusual to her. She explained that she also realized she hadn't recently seen the new jeans and blue shirt she bought him for his birthday since that day he burned clothes in the burn barrel.

The burn barrel in the backyard of Monte Seager's home (photo contained in police file)

Investigator Hagers asked Sharon if she had any other information or observations she wanted to share. Sharon did and she kept talking. Sharon stated that the day after the Beavers' murders she arrived home after working her night shift at about 7:10 a.m. She found Monte and Harry in the kitchen having breakfast. The radio was on. Sharon claimed there was an announcement of a murder in Mount Pleasant at the Beavers' house. She told Hagers that Monte mentioned at that point something about knowing Karol Beavers. Sharon explained that Monte then got up from the table and went to his bedroom, retrieved a color photograph of Karol, and showed it to her. Investigator Hagers thought this information was particularly noteworthy at the time because, based on police records, the authorities didn't release the identity of the murder victims until 9:30 a.m. on October 30, 1978. They also had not seen any photographs of Karol when they had searched the Seager's residence on April 16.

When asked if she had noticed changes in Monte's behavior after the Beavers' murders, Sharon explained that Monte had never been that interested in religion in the past. But, after the murders, she described Monte asking a lot of questions about church and religion. She claimed he also expressed more of an interest in attending church since the murders.

Based on the new information Sharon revealed in her interview with Investigator Hagers, officers obtained another search warrant authorizing officers to search the Seager's backyard and the burn barrel in an attempt to find evidence from Monte's alleged burning of clothes. The search was generally unsuccessful. Any clothes that had been burned in the barrel were completely destroyed. Although the officers found many metal clothes buttons in the ashes in the burn barrel consistent with clothes being burned there, laboratory tests couldn't provide any link to clothes Monte was possibly wearing during the Beavers' murders or anything else of evidentiary value.

On the other hand, the search warrant officers executed on Monte to obtain samples of his blood proved to be extremely valuable not only for the investigation of Monte's killing of Sue Wheelock, but also for the investigation of the Beavers' murders. Monte's blood type came back as O positive, and showed he was a secretor. The man who raped Karol, who had sucked on her breast, who had left semen in Karol, that man also had the same blood type and was also a secretor. But, so too was about 35% of the public blood Type O secretors. Karol herself was O positive, for example, and possibly a secretor.

The seizure of Monte's hair (from his head as well as pubic areas), was not helpful. The pubic hair sample obtained from Monte didn't match the single unknown pubic hair recovered from Karol's jeans. The blond hair found on her jeans was no match for Monte's black hair.

Monte's fingerprints, obtained in connection to the Sue Wheelock investigation and booking, didn't match the unknown print found on the car in the Beavers' garage.

So, although officers felt that through the investigation of the Sue Wheelock murder they had stumbled upon some additional evidence linking Monte to the murders of Clementine and Karol Beavers, it wasn't much. And it wasn't conclusive. But they knew they were on the right track and, with Monte in custody for the Wheelock murder, officers felt the community was safe and they had some time to further their investigation of his role in the Beavers' murders. If only Monte would remain in custody.

THIRTEEN

MONTE'S GREAT ESCAPE

"How did I escape? With difficulty. How did I plan this moment? With pleasure." — Alexandre Dumas, THE COUNT OF MONTE CRISTO

THE COURT APPOINTED MONTE A PUBLIC DEFENDER, Michael Shilling, to represent him in fighting the charges filed against him for assaulting and killing Sue Wheelock and for the robbery and theft at the Iris Restaurant and Iris Motel. Monte was initially held pending trial in the Henry County jail, located in the basement of the law enforcement center across the street from the courthouse in Mount Pleasant. Because Shilling's office was in Burlington, Iowa, however, Shilling requested that Monte be moved to the Des Moines County jail in Burlington so his client could be closer to him. The court granted the defense request and authorities soon moved Monte to the county jail in Burlington. Now it would be easier for Monte's attorney to work with him in preparation for trial. And, as it happens, now it would also be easier for Monte to escape.

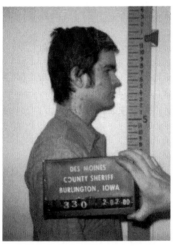

Monte Seager's booking photos from Des Moines County jail (photos from police file)

The Des Moines county jail was located in downtown Burlington, Iowa, a city located in the southeast corner of the state, not far from the borders with Illinois and Missouri. The jail occupied the top floor of a four-story brick building constituting the Des Moines County Courthouse. The building sits just a couple blocks from the Mississippi River.

There were a half dozen or so cells in the jail on either side of a long hallway, at the end of which was a window. Monte was housed alone in one of the cells. He had a bed (with a thin mattress, sheets, a couple blankets, and a pillow), a desk, a toilet, and a sink. His cell had a small window covered with bars and a steel mesh. His door was made of solid steel, with a small port that could be opened for delivering him food. There was no outside exercise yard or pen. Monte spent his entire day locked in his cell.

Part of the fourth floor also contained a small apartment where the jailor and his wife lived. The jailor's wife made all the inmates' meals. Her husband delivered the meals to the inmates three times a day through the ports in the cell doors.

Among Monte's few visitors while he was in the jail were his attorney and his little brother, Donnie. Donnie was still living in a group home in Burlington. It was easy for him to come see his big brother in jail.

The Des Moines County Jail, Burlington, Iowa (photo by author)

While Monte sat alone in the Des Moines county jail awaiting trial for killing Sue Wheelock and robbing the Iris Restaurant, his mind was focused on escaping. Eventually, he talked his 15-year-old brother Donnie into sneaking a hacksaw blade into the jail. It's not clear how Donnie snuck the hacksaw blade into the jail; Monte never told me and the investigation reports don't provide a clue. I would like to think it was baked inside a cake. However it happened, it happened. According to one of Donnie's friends, Donnie was very upset that Monte had been arrested and that officers found some coins in their father's house that police thought tied Monte to the crime. Donnie felt his brother was being set up and was apparently quite willing to help his brother escape.

In any event, Monte's stepmother, Sharon, had somehow learned about the escape plan and had warned the jail staff. For a few days after receiving the tip, jail officials searched Monte's cell daily, looking for a hacksaw blade. But they never found it, and concluded it was an unfounded rumor. It wasn't. Monte had hidden the hacksaw blade above the door to his cell.

Each night, when everyone else was asleep and no one was looking, Monte retrieved the hacksaw blade and used it to slowly cut through the deadbolt on his jail cell door. He cut the bolt from the bottom in such a way that the jailers couldn't see from the top that it had been nearly cut all the way through. When the jailers opened and shut the door each day, it appeared to work normally. But all Monte had to do when the time came to escape was pull hard on his door and it would snap off the deadbolt. Monte then waited for the right time.

In the early morning hours of August 19, 1979, at about 1:00 a.m., Monte made good his escape. He pulled hard on his cell door, snapping off the deadbolt, and just walked out of his cell. Monte slipped quietly down to the end of the corridor between the cells until he reached the window at the end of the hall. The window was covered with some thin metal bars, but he was able to bend them far enough apart to slip through the opening. The jail would later fix this flaw, as they would with the deadbolts, but it was too late to stop Monte.

Des Moines County jail window, modified with steel mesh (photo by author)

Once Monte separated the bars, he opened the window. Then, using a rope he had meticulously spliced together from strips of cloth torn from his blankets, Monte scaled down the side of the four and a half-story building, having tied one end of his make-shift rope to a radiator located conveniently right below the window. The makeshift rope wasn't quite long enough, though, and stopped short about a story above the ground. When he reached the end of the rope, Monte just let go and dropped to the ground, right outside the sheriff's office door. He must have made a loud noise when he landed, but no one heard or saw him.

Monte scaled down this side of the building to escape (photo by author)

Monte had done it. He had broken out of a jail. He was free. It was the first time in the 40-year history of the jail that anyone had escaped.

Once he reached the ground, Monte ran. A few blocks away, in the light of a waning crescent moon, Monte found and stole a bicycle. He rode the bike through the night, far out to the edge of the city, until he came across a farm with a barn. He slid the bike inside the barn and hid out in the barn the rest of the night, sleeping for a couple hours.

When Monte awoke the following morning, he wheeled the stolen bike from the barn and rode on a little ways, but soon came across a church not far away. He ditched the bicycle and strolled through the parking lot while church was in service, looking over the cars in the lot. Monte found several with keys still in the cars (this was small town, rural America, back in a time when crime was less rampant, and people were more trusting). Monte thought carefully about his choices. Though there were nicer cars he could've stolen, he chose to steal a 1977 red Toyota because he reasoned it would be more dependable and use less gas.

Once Monte stole the car, he took off driving with no particular destination in mind. He just needed to get away, to escape. First he drove south to Missouri, then eventually down through Kansas, Colorado, New Mexico, and eventually on to Arizona. To pay for food and gas along the way, he burglarized homes and businesses ("committed B&Es" in his terms) stealing money, jewelry, firearms, and anything else of value he came across.

The first home he burglarized, the day after he escaped from the jail, happened to belong to a Missouri state trooper who lived just outside of Jefferson City. Monte didn't know it was a cop's home when he broke into the house, but once inside he took advantage of it to steal a .22 caliber rifle and shotgun, ammunition, smoke grenades, and the trooper's badge. He also stole a television, food, clothes, and cash.

Then Monte drove on. He would repeat this pattern several times. When he ran out of money, he burglarized again. Monte burglarized a home in Durango, Colorado, and another in Santa Fe, New Mexico. From those homes he stole more food, cash, electronics, clothes, cameras, and a .22 caliber pistol. He stole whatever he needed, and whatever he thought he could sell to raise cash. When he came across pawn shops along the way, he would stop in and try to sell some of his stolen goods.

Monte committed his last known burglary on September 11, 1979. On that evening, he broke into a home in Flagstaff, Arizona, while the homeowners were out to dinner. He ransacked the place, stealing cash, jewelry, a camera, an electric razor, clothes, and other personal belongings. Monte helped himself to food and four bottles of wine as well. He also stole several weapons, including knives, a .330 magnum caliber rifle with a scope, a .30-.30 caliber rifle, a .38 caliber revolver, and a .45 caliber pistol, along with ammunition for all the weapons. Then he got back on the road.

A few days later, late in the evening of September 13, 1979, about a month after he escaped from the jail in

Burlington, Iowa, Monte was driving between Flagstaff and Kingman, Arizona. State Trooper Dean Couch was working radar on Route 93 north of Kingman that evening when he clocked Monte's red Toyota traveling at 62 miles an hour in an area posted for 55. Trooper Couch pulled out in his squad car to stop the car and issue the driver a citation for speeding. After following Monte a short distance, the trooper flipped on the emergency lights on the top of his patrol car, signaling Monte to stop. Monte complied, pulling over to the side of the road. Monte had the .45 caliber pistol handy, within easy reach, above the driver's side visor.

Trooper Couch stepped out of his patrol car and approached Monte's car cautiously. Monte waited until the trooper had walked all the way up to his driver's side window. But right when the trooper began to speak, Monte threw the car in gear and floored it. Monte fled down the highway in the increasing darkness, without his headlights on, at a high rate of speed. He would later tell me when I interviewed him in prison that on many occasions before while he was on the run, officers had attempted to stop him and he had successfully run from them using this risky maneuver. He figured it would work again. This time, it didn't.

Trooper Couch was particularly tenacious and a very skilled driver. When Monte fled from him, Trooper Couch sprinted back to his squad car, jumped in, and sped after Monte. He stayed on Monte's tail for miles, calling over the radio for backup. Soon, two other officers joined in the pursuit. Monte fled at speeds of up to 110 miles an hour, but the cops stayed behind him. At one point Monte threw a smoke grenade out the window of his car in an attempt to elude the officers. The highway was soon covered in red smoke, causing the officers to reduce their speed to avoid crashing. By the time the officers got through the smoke, they had temporarily lost sight of Monte's car.

As Monte approached the Hoover Dam in Northwest Arizona, the officers had spied Monte's car again and were back in pursuit, but they were far behind him. Then Monte suddenly pulled off the highway and fled down a gravel road. A waxing Gibbous moon shed just enough light for Monte to see the outline of the gravel road ahead of him. But the gravel threw up a cloud of dust behind him as he fled, further obscuring the officers' view and forcing them to again slow their pursuit. After a short distance, Monte had far outpaced the cops chasing him by this risky maneuver.

But just a few minutes later, when Monte tried to turn down another road, he lost control of the car. The right front corner slammed into the railing of a cattle guard. The car came to a sudden stop. Monte wasn't injured, but the car was totaled and completely inoperable now.

Monte jumped out of the car, grabbed the .45 caliber pistol and his backpack, and took off down the road. At some point along the route he either dropped or threw the .38 caliber revolver away. He left the rest of his arsenal and other stolen property in the car. But he still had the .45 caliber pistol.

The officers chasing Monte eventually came upon

Monte's abandoned, wrecked car, but Monte was nowhere to be seen. Officers saw an empty box of .45 caliber bullets lying next to the abandoned car, though. When officers ran a check on the Iowa license plate on Monte's car, they discovered it was stolen and likely driven by one Monte Wendell Seager, wanted for escape and murder. A routine stop for a speeding citation had taken a dramatic turn. The officers ratcheted up the urgency level of the search for the driver of the Toyota, Monte Wendell Seager.

A short time later, an officer driving down a nearby highway called out over the radio that he saw a hitchhiker walking down the highway. The other officers who had been chasing Monte replied that there hadn't been a hitch-hiker on that highway just minutes before and concluded the hitchhiker was very likely their suspect. They advised the officer to detain the hiker "with the utmost caution."

The officer stopped Monte at gunpoint. Monte didn't resist. The officer patted Monte down, but didn't find any weapons on him. He then placed Monte in the back seat of his squad car. The officer took custody of Monte's back-pack and placed it in the front seat. When officers searched the backpack later, they found the loaded .45 caliber handgun inside.

The officer drove Monte back to the scene of the aban-doned, wrecked Toyota. Once there, the officers checked Monte's shoes against shoeprints made in the dirt near the abandoned car. They matched. Officers also obtained a description over the radio of the Monte Wendell Seager wanted for escape and murder back in Iowa. That description matched Monte, especially the description of severe acne on his face and shoulders.

The officers then confronted Monte, who immediately admitted his identity. He admitted he was the driver of the Toyota and had been fleeing from the police. Officers placed him under arrest and advised him of his Constitutional rights. Monte waived his right to remain silent and confessed to committing the burglary in Flagstaff. He told them he had also committed several other burglaries while he had been on the lam. He described for the officers how he had escaped from the jail in Iowa. When questioned about the pending charges in Iowa, however, Monte admitted only to burglarizing a room in the Iris Motel. He vehemently denied having murdered Sue Wheelock.

Meanwhile, the officers had been searching Monte's car and found it full of assorted personal property, including many weapons and types of ammunition. In all, Monte had been armed with three handguns, three rifles, and a shotgun, along with several knives. Officers never found the .38 caliber revolver Monte had ditched. Officers were later able to connect many of the belongings in the car to the numerous burglaries Monte had committed while on the run.

After Monte was caught in Arizona, Iowa authorities charged Monte with escape from the jail in Burlington. State authorities in Arizona and Missouri also charged Monte for some of the burglaries he had committed. The authorities held him in Arizona pending resolution of charges there. While awaiting trial on those charges, Monte unsuccessfully tried to escape from an Arizona jail.

Thereafter, the authorities held Monte in a maximum security facility. In the meantime, Iowa authorities started the legal process for extraditing Monte back to Iowa to stand trial on the Sue Wheelock murder charge.

Monte Seager on escape status (photo by author of clipping from the Mount Pleasant News)

In November 1979, Monte finally pled guilty to burglary of a residence in Flagstaff, Arizona, where he had made off with some jewelry and firearms, among other property. On December 17, 1979, an Arizona judge sentenced Monte to five years in prison for that burglary.

Officers later interviewed some of the inmates serving time in the same Arizona jail where Monte was housed pending resolution of his cases there and his extradition back to Iowa. According to these inmates, Monte claimed the only crime he committed back in Iowa was breaking into a motel room. He denied killing anyone. He told the other inmates that he knew officers were investigating him for the murder of a waitress, and told one inmate that he was worried that other inmates would tell on him. So he mostly kept his mouth shut.

In jail, Monte kept to himself. Occasionally, he played checkers with another inmate, but he spent most of his days sleeping. During the entire time he was held in the Arizona jail, Monte didn't receive a single phone call, letter, or visitor, and he didn't mail out any letters or try to call anyone. Monte was a loner, and alone.

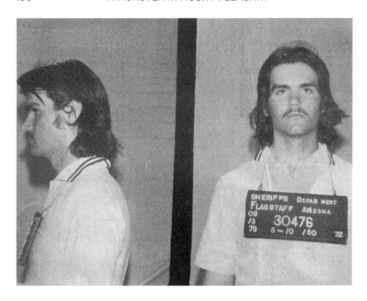

*Monte Seager's booking photos from Flagstaff,
Arizona (photo by author of booking photos contained
in police file)*

Monte initially fought extradition back to Iowa, but
eventually lost that fruitless legal challenge. In January
1980, after being sentenced on the Arizona burglary
charge, Monte was finally extradited back to Iowa under
heightened security to answer for the charges arising out of
his murder of Sue Wheelock.

News staff photo by Bill Epperheimer

Sheriff Dick Droz, right, Monday morning escorted Monte Seager to the Henry County courthouse for a hearing. Seager is being held in the Des Moines County jail.

2-11-80

Announcement of Monte's return to stand trial for killing Sue Wheelock (photo by Mount Pleasant News)

Once Monte was back in Iowa, the public defender from Burlington continued to represent him. The trial was rescheduled and months passed as the parties prepared. Eventually, Monte's attorney was able to negotiate a sweetheart plea deal with the county attorney, Mike Riepe, on the Wheelock-related charges.

On June 3, 1980, a little less than six months after returning to Iowa, Monte pled guilty to the reduced charge of murder in the second degree for killing Sue Wheelock, theft in the second degree, and burglary in the second degree. This was a huge break for Monte. A murder committed in the course of another felony, like a burglary, constituted murder in the first degree under Iowa law. Murder in the first degree carried a mandatory sentence of life in prison without the possibility of parole. The evidence of Monte's guilt for burglarizing the Iris Restaurant and killing Sue Wheelock was overwhelming. He had a history of stealing from the restaurant, he admitted breaking into the motel room the night of the attack, his shoes matched the shoeprints left in Sue's blood, and, most important, the blood on his pants matched Sue Wheelock's blood type. His daring escape from custody only cemented his fate; nothing screams guilt more than running. Nevertheless, County Attorney Riepe cut the plea deal with Monte, allowing Monte to evade a life sentence. Perhaps it was because the County Attorney had no experience trying murder cases.

At his guilty plea hearing, Monte claimed he had entered the restaurant to steal liquor and food and was surprised when Wheelock walked up behind him. He confessed that he struck Sue Wheelock in the head with a stick and bottles. He admitted taking Sue's purse, along with cash from the restaurant. During the plea hearing, Monte also admitted breaking into Room 26 in the adjoining motel to steal a television, but said he left without it. Monte never mentioned anyone else participating in the crimes. He claimed to act alone.

On June 26, 1980, Monte's case came on for sentencing. The authorities remained jittery about this dangerous prisoner who had already escaped once, and had attempted another escape in Arizona. So, just prior to the sentencing hearing, law enforcement officers required all members of the press and the public who had gathered to attend the hearing to exit the courtroom and be subject to a search by law enforcement personnel before they were allowed back into the courtroom. This included searching members of Sue Wheelock's family.

Once officers were certain the courtroom was secure, the sentencing hearing proceeded. When it came time at the sentencing hearing for the offender to give an allocution, Monte declined to make a statement. The judge sentenced Monte to 40 years in prison for the charges arising from Sue Wheelock's murder. Under Iowa law at the time, Monte would be eligible for parole in about 15 years.

Before Monte was shipped off to prison, he still had to resolve the escape charge pending against him in Burlington. Surprisingly, Monte contested the escape charge and demanded a trial, even though the evidence was overwhelming that he escaped. Nevertheless, Monte waived a jury trial. He was tried in Burlington, Iowa before Judge Harlan Bainter, the father of one of my high school classmates. Judge Bainter found Monte guilty of escape, of course, after a very short trial. At a hearing a few months later following the bench trial, Judge Bainter tacked five more years on Monte's sentence for his escape from the jail in Burlington.

With a 40-year sentence for murdering Sue and the related charges, a five-year sentence for escape, together with the five year sentence for the burglary in Arizona, Monte faced a total of 50 years in prison. With the usual built-in time reductions for good behavior in prison, Monte would serve less than half that time. His sentence was set to expire in January 1999. Monte could be paroled, however, before his prison term expired. This prison sentence gave law enforcement officers breathing room to continue the investigation into Monte's involvement in the Beavers' murders. But the clock was ticking.

FOURTEEN

BEAVERS' MURDER INVESTIGATION (CONTINUED)

Nothing matters but the facts. Without them, the science of criminal investigation is nothing more than a guessing game.
—Blake Edwards

WHILE MONTE WAS PENDING CHARGES FOR THE Wheelock murder, while he was on the run from the law in the late summer of 1979, and after he had been captured, convicted, and sentenced for the burglaries, Wheelock's murder, and his escape, law enforcement officers continued to investigate Monte's possible involvement in the Beavers' murders.

Investigator Hagers and other officers had immediately recognized the importance of the .22 caliber rifle they happened to observe during the April 1979 search of the Seager residence when they were looking for evidence of Monte's involvement in the attack on Sue Wheelock. They realized then that it could be evidence tying Monte to the Beavers' murders, but the search warrant didn't authorize officers to seize a gun because Sue Wheelock wasn't attacked with a firearm. So, in June 1979, while Monte was sitting in the Burlington jail awaiting trial for the murder of Sue Wheelock, officers initiated efforts to gain custody of what they suspected might be the weapon used to murder Clementine and Karol.

The officers' first attempt to gain custody of the rifle was to approach Harry Seager and simply request that he voluntarily surrender Monte's rifle to the authorities. Harry refused. Harry told Investigator Hagers that Monte's attorney had instructed him that if the authorities wanted to do any more searching, Harry should make them produce a warrant. So, Harry politely declined to surrender the rifle without a warrant.

Turned down by Harry, Investigator Hagers next focused his efforts on obtaining a search warrant for evidence that Monte was involved in the Beavers' murders. Hagers reviewed all the evidence the authorities had at that stage pointing toward Monte's involvement in the Beavers' murders. Hagers decided he had enough evidence to seek a search warrant for such evidence. Hagers drafted an application for a search warrant to search for evidence tying Monte to the murders, but at first, Hagers didn't seek permission to seize Monte's rifle. He recognized he didn't yet have enough evidence to establish probable cause to believe Monte's rifle was the murder weapon. Under the Fourth Amendment to the United States Constitution, an officer can search a residence and seize evidence only if the officer can persuade a judge that there is probable cause, that there is a reasonable basis to believe evidence of the crime is present in the place to be searched. But officers must also show probable cause that the items they wish to seize constitutes evidence of the crime.

Here, Hagers thought there was enough information tying Monte to the murders to search the residence for some evidence, but not enough information to seize the rifle as evidence of the crime. In particular, Fran Worth had recently mentioned to law enforcement officers that she had once seen Monte wearing a large belt buckle at work, and officers still believed that the murderer might have left the impression of a belt buckle in blood on Karol's T-shirt. On the other hand, officers had no basis to tell the judge that they believed the murderer used a rifle. It didn't make sense. It seemed much more likely the killer used a handgun, specifically a revolver. Investigator Hagers hoped that a search for other evidence linking Monte to the Beavers' murders might turn up enough of a connection to the rifle to persuade the judge to issue another search warrant to seize the rifle.

Investigator Hagers took his search warrant application to a Henry County judge. The judge granted the warrant, which authorized officers to search and seize evidence that might tie Monte to the Beavers' murders, including authorizing officers to seize articles of clothing and belt buckles, but it didn't authorize them to seize Monte's rifle.

On July 11, 1979, officers executed the search warrant

at the Seager's home, this time looking for evidence tied to the Beavers' murders. The officers seized, among other things, camera film, belt buckles, a partial box of CCI .22 caliber ammunition, and two pairs of women's white panties found between the mattresses of the bed in the room where Monte slept. Officers didn't find a large belt buckle like they had hoped to find, the type of buckle that might have left an impression in the blood on Karol's yellow T-shirt. During this search, officers again saw Monte's rifle, but didn't seize it—they couldn't seize it—because the search warrant didn't authorize them to do so.

After gaining some additional evidence from the July 11 search, particularly finding ammunition that matched the type used in the murders, Investigator Hagers decided that perhaps they finally had enough evidence to seek a warrant to seize Monte's rifle. The affidavit Investigator Hagers typed up in support of the search warrant recited all the evidence the police had gathered up to that time linking Monte to the Beavers' murders. It wasn't much. Officers could establish that Monte knew Karol and had a class with her, that he was a Type O secreter, and the murderer and rapist was also a Type O secretor. Officers could establish that Monte was seen by his stepmother burning clothes the day after the murders. From the July 11 search, officers could now establish that Monte was in possession of ammunition that could match that used in the murders. From their own observations during the prior searches and Monte's parents' statements, officers could establish that Monte owned a .22 caliber rifle. They could show forensic analysis established that the weapon used to murder Clementine and Karol was a .22 caliber firearm, and that a Mossberg rifle was one possible match for the murder weapon. And, authorities now had evidence that Monte had since murdered a waitress.

When Investigator Hagers presented the search warrant application to the judge for approval, the judge hesitated to authorize seizure of Monte's rifle. He commented that the evidence seemed very thin linking Monte to the Beavers' murders. At this point, Investigator Hagers decided to add some additional facts to the affidavit in handwriting. He added that Karol was known to always wear a heart shaped locket her mother Clementine had given her for her birthday, but the necklace wasn't found on Karol's body or anywhere in the house. He also wrote that back during the April 1979 search of the Seager's residence when officers were looking for evidence of Monte's connection to the Wheelock murder, Sheriff Richard Droz happened to have seen a necklace that matched the description of the one that Karol was known to wear. Investigator Hagers wrote that Sheriff Droz had seen the necklace in a metal box in Monte's room.

The judge reviewed the revised affidavit in support of the search warrant with the added hand-written paragraph. Though the evidence was still weak, with this additional information the judge found probable cause to believe that Monte's rifle could constitute evidence of his involvement in the Beavers' murders. The judge granted the search warrant and authorized Investigator Hagers permission to seize the weapon.

Page from affidavit in support of search warrant bearing Investigator Hagers' handwritten addendum to the facts (photo by author of search warrant affidavit contained in court file)

Finally, on July 26, 1979, Investigator Hagers and other officers returned to the Seager's residence and executed the new search warrant, seizing Monte's .22 caliber Mossberg rifle. Upon taking possession of the weapon, the officers immediately examined it more closely and noted that the serial number had been filed off. That was some indication of guilt in the sense that it suggested Monte removed the serial number to make the weapon harder to trace back to him. All gun dealers must document the sale of firearms by serial number. Without a serial number, law enforcement wouldn't be able to directly tie Monte to the purchase of the firearm. Nevertheless, seizing the weapon from Monte's home, and his parents' admissions about it being Monte's gun, would be enough to show it was his weapon. The more difficult task was establishing that Monte's weapon was the one used to kill Clementine and Karol. That would take an expert. So, the Mount Pleasant Police Department shipped the weapon to the BCI laboratory near Des Moines, requesting that a ballistics expert examine the firearm to determine if it was used to kill the Beavers.

The inside of rifle barrels have lines cut into them in a spiral pattern (called rifling, hence the term for such long guns). The lines cut into the barrel are called grooves and the part not cut is referred to as the lands of the barrel. When a firearm is discharged, it causes the gunpowder in the bullet cartridge to explode and send the bullet down the barrel. A lead bullet expands slightly as it proceeds down the barrel. The softer lead of the bullet presses into the grooves cut in the steel barrel. The spiraled grooves cut into the barrel cause the bullet to spin as the bullet speeds down the barrel and out the end, propelled by the explosion of the gunpowder. That spinning action is what makes a bullet accurate, just like the spin a quarterback puts on a football makes the throw more accurate. Because of minor imperfections during the manufacturing processes and the natural marring of the barrel caused by continued use and wear of firearms, barrels invariably leave unique markings on spent bullets.

When officers seize a weapon they believe was used in a crime, the procedure then is to have an expert conduct a ballistics test of the firearm. This involves the expert discharging or shooting new bullets from the firearm, firing the bullets into a soft material, like a water tank, to capture the bullets undamaged. These are called the exemplar bullets. The expert then compares the markings left on the exemplar bullets from the laboratory against the markings left on the spent bullets recovered from the crime scene. Under a microscope, a ballistics expert will closely compare the markings left by the lands and grooves and any other minor imperfections in the barrel of the suspect weapon on the exemplar bullets discharged from that weapon against the markings left on the spent bullets from the crime scene. If the unique markings are the same, a ballistics expert can opine that the suspect weapon was likely used in the crime.

When the BCI ballistics expert conducted the forensic examination on Monte's rifle, however, he quickly realized he would be stymied in trying to perform a ballistics comparison with this weapon. On close examination, the expert discovered that someone had been one step ahead of the police. When the expert examined the inside of the barrel of Monte's rifle, he discovered that it appeared that someone had recently taken a screwdriver or some other sharp metal instrument and had intentionally and repeatedly scratched and marred the inside of the barrel. The expert determined that Monte's Mossberg rifle had eight lands and grooves with a righthand twist, but the apparently recent alteration of the inside of the barrel would call into question a ballistics comparison. The scratching of the barrel would cause any exemplar bullets now shot from Monte's weapon to have slightly different markings left on them than would have been present at the time of the murders, before someone had intentionally altered the inside of the rifle barrel.

That was probably why Monte never bothered destroying or disposing of the murder weapon. Recall that just a couple weeks after he was first interviewed about the Beavers' murders in November of 1978, Monte checked out the *Crime Scientists* book from the Mount Pleasant High School library. That book included a chapter on ballistics tests on firearms. Having intentionally marred the inside of the rifle's barrel, Monte knew that if the police tried to conduct a ballistics comparison, any exemplar bullet shot from his weapon would not perfectly match a bullet retrieved from either victim.

In the end, the ballistics examination was ultimately only somewhat fruitful, meaning the examiner could testify that the bullet retrieved from Clementine's head had markings on it similar to those of bullets test-fired from Monte's gun. He could testify that the bullet used to kill Clementine was shot from a rifle with eight lands and grooves with a righthand twist. But that was about all he could say. He couldn't say it was a perfect match. The expert could not definitely opine that Monte's rifle was the murder weapon. There were other slightly different markings on the exemplar bullets, likely from the intentional marring of the barrel, that were inconsistent with markings recovered from the bullet shot into Clementine's head. These inconsistencies would provide some basis for a good defense attorney to challenge the assertion that Monte's rifle was, in fact, the murder weapon.

While all these frustrating efforts to investigate the Beavers' murders continued, the saga of Monte's prosecution for the Wheelock murder and the aftermath moved forward to its conclusion. A little more than a year after Monte had killed Sue, after he had been charged, escaped, been captured, convicted in Arizona of burglary, convicted in Henry County Iowa of the Wheelock murder and burglary of the Iris Restaurant and Motel, and convicted in Des Moines County of escape, the State of Iowa finally sent him to prison to serve his sentence. It was there that officers traveled to interview him once again.

On July 1, 1980, officers interviewed Monte for the second time about the murders of Clementine and Karol. This interview took place at the Iowa State Penitentiary, in Fort Madison, where Monte was serving his sentences. The ancient and decrepit penitentiary was built in 1839, four years before Mount Pleasant was founded and seven years before Iowa became a state. The prison was located at the edge of the Fort Madison business district, within sight of the Mississippi River in southeast Iowa, about 35 miles from Mount Pleasant. The prison had imposing stone walls, topped by barbed wire and guard towers. The prison has since been shuttered, replaced by a modern prison on the outskirts of town.

When the officers sat down with Monte this second time, but before they questioned him, officers advised Monte of his constitutional rights, as required by the

Supreme Court's *Miranda* decision. Monte acknowledged he understood his rights and waived them, agreeing to speak with the police without a lawyer present.

During the interrogation, Monte continued adamantly to deny any involvement in the Beavers' murders. He claimed he couldn't remember now, two years later, what all he did the day of the murders other than he remembered he was watching television that night. He told the officers he thought he may have worked at the Iris Restaurant from 10:00 a.m. to 4:00 p.m. the day of the murders (though it turned out he was mistaken in that recollection).

During this interview, unlike what he told officers in his first interview, Monte admitted leaving his house twice on the night of the murders. Back when he was first interviewed in November 1978, Monte claimed he never left the house at all that night. This time around, the officers pressed him on his father's recollection of hearing Monte leaving the home after his stepmother went to work. Monte recalled during this interrogation that he did leave the house twice, but he claimed he only left the house briefly both times, just long enough to check on and water some marijuana plants he had growing in the backyard. He couldn't explain why his father didn't hear him come back into the house.

Other than admitting that he briefly left the house the night of the murders, Monte's story during the second interview was largely the same one he told officers when first interviewed in November 1978. Monte claimed he watched the *Battleship Galactica* show and the movie about the airplane crash and then he went to bed before his stepmother left for work a little after 10:00 p.m. Monte described his sleeping situation, explaining that he was sleeping on the couch in the living room at that time. Monte continued to claim he learned about the murders for the first time the following morning when he arrived at school and overheard another student speaking to his speech teacher, Ms. Vincent, about the murders (which was inconsistent with Ms. Vincent's recollection that it was Monte who told her about the murders).

The officers focused a little more in their questioning about how Monte used his rifle. Monte continued to claim all he ever did with the rifle was shoot at paper targets. Monte described how he and his little brother Donnie would sometimes shoot targets at the city dump. He even drew a map for the officers to show them the location in the dump where he and Donnie shot at targets. The interview ended shortly after Monte drew the map for them.

After the interview, the officers realized that evidence from Monte's target practice could potentially be key. If, by chance, officers could recover spent bullets from the target practice area, those bullets might still have markings on them from the barrel of Monte's rifle from the time before he scratched and marred the inside of the barrel to hamper ballistics comparisons. The laboratory couldn't use the exemplar bullets shot out of Monte's weapon now to use for perfect comparison purposes because Monte had marred the inside of the barrel. The defense would be able to point out some minor differences in the bullets due to the new marring. But, if the officers could recover some intact bullets from the target location where Monte and Donnie practiced shooting the rifle, those bullets wouldn't have those same minor defects on them. Then the laboratory might be able to use the bullets Monte and Donnie shot at targets in the past as exemplars to compare against the bullets used to kill Karol and Clementine to see if they were consistent.

To pursue this line of investigation, officers met up with Donnie Seager the following day to ask him about the target practice. Donnie was now living with his father, Harry, in Mount Pleasant. Donnie confirmed that he and Monte shot at targets at the city dump. Donnie agreed to travel to the dump with the officers to help them locate the exact spot where they shot at targets. Once at the dump, Donnie was able to find and identify the location where he and Monte shot paper targets thumbtacked onto poles that were part of an old, now abandoned, wooden railroad trestle. The officers observed that the creosote-soaked wooden pole, the thickness of a telephone pole, was riddled with bullet holes.

Investigator Hagers returned to his home, retrieved his personal chain saw, and traveled back to the dump. There, he cut out a large section of the support pole that contained the bullet holes. Then, back at the office, he carefully and methodically removed the slugs from the wood, being careful not to scratch or mar the bullets as he removed them. Investigator Hagers first took a sledge hammer and an awl to the piece of wood, splitting it apart, piece by piece. Then he used a pocket knife to carefully tease and pry the bullets out of the wood. Hagers was able to recover 38 bullets from the cut-out section of bridge support. Hagers then sent those spent bullets to the forensic crime laboratory near Des Moines for analysis and hoped for the best.

A ballistics expert at the crime lab examined the rifling markings of the spent bullets that Monte and Donnie shot into the targets at the dump against the rifling markings left on the bullets recovered from Karol and Clementine's heads. Many of the bullets recovered from the target practice were too marred and mangled from impact to be used for comparison purposes, but at least two were in pretty good shape. Similarly, the bullet recovered from Karol's head was too mangled to allow accurate comparison, but the bullet shot into the back of Clementine's head wasn't as badly damaged and could be used for comparison purposes.

Under a microscope, the ballistics expert examined the markings on the bullet recovered from Clementine's head against similar markings left on the bullets Monte and Donnie shot into the targets at the dump. The expert concluded that the markings were identical. In a written report, the ballistics expert opined that the firearm used to shoot bullets into the targets at the dump behind Saunders Park was the same firearm used to shoot the bullet that killed Clementine Beavers. This was critically important evidence. But before officers could act on it, there were two other developments that delayed them in charging Monte with murdering Clementine and Karol.

Sometime later in that summer of 1980, Sharon

Gaylord came to the Mount Pleasant Police department for a second time, again in tears, asking to speak with investigators. She said she had yet more information to get off her chest. She told them that she had recently visited Monte in prison in Fort Madison. She explained Monte told her about how the police were still investigating him about the Beavers' murders and that they had been to the prison to question him. Monte then told Sharon that he had left a parka at the house before he was arrested in 1979. He told Sharon to find the parka and get rid of it.

Sharon confessed to the officers that when she returned home after visiting Monte in prison, she searched the house and found the parka that Monte described. She told the officers she saw brown stains on the front of the parka and agreed with the officers that it was possible the stains could have been blood, but said she couldn't say for sure. Sharon explained that she put the parka in a box and took the box to the town dump where she threw it in the trash. The police were clearly interested in the parka; it fit with the description of the man seen walking in the neighborhood wearing a parka the night of the murders, with the man who said his name was Andy Collins. But Sharon explained that she had taken the parka to the dump several weeks ago. By the time Sharon told the police about the parka, it was way too late to ever recover it from the city dump.

Then, on August 24, 1980, a middle-aged man named Dick Keller shot and killed his wife and her mother with a .22 caliber handgun as the two sat in a car in front of their house. It turned out that the murders were the product of a domestic dispute. But the Keller house happened to be located less than a half block away from the Beavers' residence. Given the proximity of the Keller house to the Beavers' home, officers were briefly distracted from the focus on Monte while they investigated the outside possibility that Keller could have been involved in the Beavers' murders. Soon, though, investigators eliminated Keller as a suspect in the Beavers' murders when his alibi checked out and forensics revealed he was of the wrong blood type to have raped Karol.

Finally, in January 1981, officers took stock of the evidence they had showing that Monte Seager killed Clementine and Karol Beavers. Through their long-term investigation, officers had collected a fair amount of evidence pointing to Monte as the murderer: (1) saliva left on Karol Beavers' breast and semen recovered from her vagina were from an "O" type secretor and Monte was an "O" type secretor; (2) Monte's father said Monte had used CCI .22 caliber non-magnum ammunition in the Mossberg rifle, the same type of ammunition used in the murders, the same type officers later found in Monte's house; (3) Monte's brother, Donnie, confirmed that he and Monte had shot the rifle at the park and the city dump; (4) ballistics tests on bullets recovered from poles in the city dump behind Saunders Park showed that three of the bullets were of the same type as those recovered from the murder victims (CCI .22 caliber long-rifle non-magnum) and the ballistics expert opined that one of those bullets had been fired from the same gun that fired the bullet taken from Clementine Beavers' head;

(5) Monte's stepmother reported that Monte came home early from school the day after the murders claiming he was sick and she saw him burn something that afternoon that looked like clothing, and later Monte had his stepmother dispose of a parka; (6) Monte provided officers with a map showing exactly where in the dump behind Saunders Park he and his brother shot targets; (7) Monte knew Karol and they had a class together; and (8) Monte lived near the Beavers' home. It wasn't an overwhelming case, but it was enough. The agents took their case to the county attorney and pressed him to charge Monte Seager with the murders of Clementine and Karol Beavers.

FIFTEEN
PROSECUTION AND SUPPRESSION

"Our cases have consistently recognized that unbending application of the exclusionary sanction to enforce ideals of governmental rectitude would impede unacceptably the truth-finding functions of judge and jury."
United States v. Payner, 447 U.S. 727, 734 (1980).

HENRY COUNTY ATTORNEY MIKE RIEPE SPENT months reviewing the evidence and pondering whether he had enough evidence, evidence beyond a reasonable doubt, to convict Monte of murdering Clementine and Karol Beavers. At Riepe's request, the State Attorney General's Office assigned one of his Assistant Attorney Generals, Michael Jordan, to assist Riepe in the case. The two prosecutors reviewed the evidence and consulted with the law enforcement officers. Finally, on August 10, 1981, they decided to pull the trigger on the prosecution. On behalf of the State of Iowa, Riepe charged Monte with the first degree murders of Clementine and Karol Beavers. The court issued a warrant for Monte's arrest.

Authorities brought Monte out of prison to make an appearance in the Henry County courthouse. At his initial appearance on the charges, Monte pled not guilty. The court appointed two attorneys, John Logan and Frank Nidey, state public defenders who officed in Cedar Rapids, Iowa, to represent Monte in the Beavers' murders case. On Monte's behalf, the attorneys waived Monte's speedy trial rights and the court scheduled the trial to take place in about six months.

In the meantime, Logan and Nidey quickly got to work reviewing the government's evidence. They also took the depositions of several of the key potential witnesses, meaning they questioned the witnesses under oath with a court reporter taking down their testimony. After a few months of this work, Monte's attorneys filed motions to suppress evidence found during the investigation.

The "suppression of evidence" is a phrase used to describe a court ruling that bars the government from using evidence when the court finds the government violated the defendant's constitutional rights in obtaining the evidence. This remedy isn't expressly provided for in the Constitution. Indeed, the Constitution is silent about the remedy for government violations of an offender's constitutional rights in a criminal investigation. In 1914, however, the United States Supreme Court determined that the proper remedy is to suppress the evidence, or, in other words, to bar the government from using the very evidence it obtained through the violation of an offender's rights. Sometimes called the exclusionary rule, its purpose is to punish the government for violating an offender's constitutional rights and to deter officers from doing so in the future.

A court may also suppress evidence—or bar its admission—if it finds that evidence is so unreliable that admission of the evidence would violate an offender's constitutional due process rights. This can occur even when the government didn't violate the constitution in seizing or obtaining the evidence. The rules of evidence are designed to protect jurors from exposure to evidence that courts deem unreliable or misleading or unfairly prejudicial, fearing that jurors could be led to convict the accused on improper grounds. In some instances, evidence may be so unreliable or so unfairly prejudicial, however, that admission of it would be deemed a violation of an offender's constitutional right to due process, as guaranteed under the Due Process Clause of the United States Constitution.

The first of the suppression motions Monte's attorneys filed sought suppression of testimony from two prospective witnesses, Sharon Gaylord and Max Beavers. These motions were premised on the theory that admission of the evidence would violate Monte's due process rights because the evidence was inherently unreliable. Both of these witnesses, at the behest of the government investigators, had undergone hypnosis in an effort to enhance their memories. This, the defense attorneys argued, made those witnesses' testimony so inherently unreliable that the judge should completely bar them from testifying at trial.

The use of hypnosis in law enforcement—forensic hypnosis—enjoyed a short-lived and ill-fated popularity beginning in the late 1950s and fading away in the early 1980s. The technique involved having a trained hypnotist persuade witnesses to focus their gaze on an object and relax their minds so as to lull the witnesses into sort of a supposed trance. Then the hypnotists would gently ask probing questions about a crime to allegedly tease out information that the witnesses' minds purportedly registered subconsciously at the time of the crime, but which the witnesses couldn't recall consciously.

Courts were skeptical of its admissibility from the beginning, but in 1968 a court found testimony based on hypnotically-induced memory admissible. This watershed ruling resulted in the spread of the use of forensic hypnosis for a period of time during the 1960s and 1970s. By 1978, many courts across the country were admitting hypnotic-induced testimony into evidence in both civil and criminal cases. Nevertheless, the criminal defense bar kept fighting its admissibility, increasingly pointing out defects in the method that rendered the so-called recovered memories unreliable.

In Monte's case, his defense attorneys argued that the hypnosis rendered the witnesses' testimony so inherently unreliable that allowing the witnesses to testify after having their memories altered by hypnosis would deprive Monte of a fair trial. At a March 30, 1982 hearing on the motion to suppress, the defense attorney called Dr. Martin

T. Orne, a recognized expert in the field of hypnosis, to testify. Dr. Orne testified generally that hypnosis wasn't a reliable or scientifically accepted means of generating accurate recollections from witnesses. He testified that the hypnotic process actually warped witnesses' perceptions of what really occurred by creating "pseudo memories."

In response, the prosecutor offered into evidence the deposition testimony transcript of D. Eric Elster, the hypnotist who had sought to enhance Max's and Sharon's memories in Monte's case. In his deposition testimony, Elster claimed hypnosis was reliable, depending on the opportunity for external corroboration of the information gleaned from the subject under hypnosis. In its written opinion, the court noted that Elster didn't directly respond to allegations that the hypnotic process created "pseudo memories" resulting in unreliable testimony.

The court found in Monte's favor on this issue. The judge concluded that as a result of the continuing effects of hypnosis on their memories, the testimony expected from these two key witnesses—Max Beavers and Sharon Gaylord—was sufficiently suspect as to be wholly unreliable. The judge ruled that neither witness would be permitted to testify at the trial. At all. About anything.

The second motion to suppress evidence related to the items seized during the search of the Seager's house on July 26, 1979, specifically Monte's Mossberg rifle. The defense attorneys alleged that the affidavit presented in support of the search warrant contained intentionally false statements. Mount Pleasant Police Investigator Gus Hagers drafted the affidavit in support of the search warrant with the help of a BCI agent. In the affidavit Investigator Hagers claimed in the last paragraph that:

During the April 16th 1979 search of the 501 S. Jefferson residence [the Seager residence], sheriff Droz observed a locket in a metal box in the upstairs bedroom similar to the one believed missing in the Beavers homicide case.

Although the rest of the affidavit was typed, that last paragraph was handwritten after the judge expressed some hesitation about whether there was a showing of probable cause.

Hagers had resigned from the police department in September 1980 and had since pursued a career in construction. When questioned about this added information during a deposition in February 1982, Hagers testified that he didn't recall talking to Sheriff Droz about the locket, so he assumed the information in that last paragraph must have come from BCI Special Agent Larry Goepel who was assisting in the drafting of the search warrant application.

At the March 30, 1982 suppression hearing, however, Hagers testified inconsistently with his prior deposition testimony. At the hearing, he testified that while he and Special Agent Goepel were preparing the warrant application, Sheriff Droz briefly entered the room and asked if a locket was missing in the Beavers' investigation. Hagers testified that when he and Droz confirmed that there was a missing locket, Sheriff Droz then revealed that in the April 1979 search of the Seager residence in connection with the Wheelock homicide investigation he had discovered a metal box that contained a heart-shaped locket. Hagers testified that he had been present during that April 1979 search when the box had been discovered by the sheriff and had viewed the contents of the box at that time. Hagers testified that he didn't personally recall seeing a locket in the box. Hagers explained he didn't initially include the information in the typed portion of the affidavit in support of the search warrant because it was inconsistent with his own memory, but decided to supplement the affidavit in handwriting at the time he appeared before a district judge seeking issuance of the warrant, relying on what Sheriff Droz had told him while Hagers and Goepel were drafting the July 1979 search warrant application.

After Hagers finished testifying at the suppression hearing, the defense attorneys called Agent Goepel to testify. Agent Goepel testified that he was aware of a missing locket in connection with the Beavers' homicides. He also testified that he vaguely recalled that Sheriff Droz briefly came into the room while he and Investigator Hagers were preparing the search warrant application. He testified that he couldn't recall, however, the substance of the conversation that took place at that time. Critically, he specifically testified that he didn't recall Sheriff Droz saying anything about having seen a heart-shaped locket during the April 1979 search of the Seager residence. In short, Agent Goepel's testimony was inconsistent with Hagers' testimony.

Then the defense attorneys called Sheriff Droz to testify at the suppression hearing. The defense attorneys had previously obtained an affidavit from Sheriff Droz denying that he had ever seen a locket during the April 1979 search of the Seager residence. In the affidavit, Sheriff Droz also denied ever having told Hagers about allegedly seeing such a locket. At the suppression hearing, Sheriff Droz affirmed that the information in the affidavit was true. The key exchange was as follows:

Q. Were you at that time or from then on or up until this year aware that any other authorities, and I'm talking about police department, DCI were, in fact, looking for a locket in connection with the Beavers' homicide?

A. Not that I can recall at all, no, sir.

Q. Can you recall them ever giving you a description of a locket for which they were looking?

A. No, sir.

Q. Can you ever recall telling any other law enforcement authorities that you had observed a locket on April 16th, 1979, during the search?

A. No, sir.

Sheriff Droz testified that the first he had learned about the fact that a locket was missing in the Beavers' homicide, or that he was claimed to have noticed a similar locket at the Seager residence, was when Monte's defense attorney informed him of these claims prior to his testifying at the suppression hearing. It also came out in his testimony that Sheriff Droz and Investigator Hagers didn't get along well and usually didn't speak directly to each other. The poor relationship between Sheriff Droz and Hagers, years in the making, could be taken two different ways. It could be seen as making it less likely that Sheriff

Droz would drop by to talk with Hagers or try to help him with the Beavers' murder investigation. On the other hand, it could also be seen as showing Sheriff Droz was biased against Hagers and would have a motive to testify in a way that would make it look like Hagers was lying.

After hearing all the testimony, the judge took the motion to suppress under advisement and a few weeks later issued a written decision granting the motion. In the written order, the judge found that Investigator Hagers' statement in the affidavit concerning the sheriff seeing the locket during the April 1979 search was deliberately false. The judge granted the defense motion to suppress all evidence from the July 26, 1979 search, including the murder weapon and any evidence derived from that evidence. Critically, that included the ballistics testing conducted showing that the bullet fired into Clementine's head had markings consistent with bullets fired from Monte's rifle.

The prosecutors immediately appealed the judge's two decisions suppressing the witnesses' hypnotically-enhanced testimony and the evidence from the July 1979 search. On appeal, the Iowa Supreme Court affirmed the district court judge's suppression of the evidence from the search of the house, affirming the finding that Investigator Hagers had lied in the affidavit in support of the warrant. The Iowa Supreme Court agreed with the district court that without that additional, false information, the warrant lacked probable cause to seize the firearm. On the other hand, the Iowa Supreme Court reversed in part the district court's suppression of the testimony by Max Beavers and Sharon

Gaylord. The Supreme Court agreed that any testimony based on memories allegedly recovered from hypnosis was unreliable and should be suppressed. Nevertheless, the Supreme Court found that the witnesses should be permitted to testify about other matters so long as they didn't testify about matters recalled only under hypnosis.[1]

The Supreme Court's ruling largely affirming the district court's orders suppressing evidence was a severe blow to the government's case. Without the murder weapon and the forensic evidence from the ballistics testing, the government's case was eviscerated. The prosecutors and law enforcement officers met to discuss the impact of the adverse court rulings and to assess whether there was any way, without the evidence the courts had suppressed, they could convince a jury beyond a reasonable doubt that Monte murdered Clementine and Karol Beavers. They concluded that their remaining evidence was too thin of a reed upon which to support the first degree murder prosecution.

So, on February 21, 1984, the State of Iowa voluntarily dismissed the charges against Monte. Without Monte's rifle in evidence, and the ballistics testing that showed that it matched the murder weapon, the prosecutors and law enforcement officers concluded that there was simply not enough evidence to convict Monte of the Beavers' murders. The dismissal of the case was made "without prejudice," however, meaning that the State of Iowa could charge Monte again with the murders in the

---

1. *State v. Seager*, 341 N.W.2d 420, 432 (Iowa 1983).

future, if investigators were later able to develop other, additional evidence sufficient to prove Monte's guilt without using any of the evidence the court had suppressed.

A few months later in 1984, the State of Iowa filed an application for an order from the court determining the disposition of the seized property, specifically Monte's rifle and ammunition. In other words, the State wanted a court order telling it what to do with Monte's rifle, the rifle the courts found the government had taken in violation of Monte's constitutional rights. Since it had been returned from the laboratory after the ballistics testing, Monte's rifle had remained in the evidence locker at the Highway Patrol office where the resident BCI agent had his office. Neither Monte nor anyone else had made a claim of ownership of the firearm or sought its return. Finding no claims of ownership or claims for return of the property, the district court ordered Monte's rifle and ammunition forfeited to the State of Iowa for disposition as provided for under Iowa law. Thereafter, Monte's rifle sat in storage along with other evidence in the evidence vault at the highway patrol office in Mount Pleasant, awaiting another day when, possibly, the evidence could be used against Monte to hold him responsible for slaying Clementine and Karol. That day would eventually come. But for now, Monte had evaded justice.

SIXTEEN
ROUND TWO

"Perseverance, secret of all triumphs." – Victor Hugo

FOR ALMOST A DECADE AFTER THE SUPPRESSION OF the murder weapon as evidence, the Beavers' murder investigation languished. While Monte served his sentences for killing Sue Wheelock, escape, and burglary of homes, as each passing year brought Monte closer and closer to release from prison, the investigation into the brutal murders of Clementine and Karol Beavers moved no closer to resolution. The Beavers' murders became a cold case. And with each passing year, it became colder.

Then, in early 1993, the Iowa Bureau of Criminal Investigation assigned Special Agent Ron Mower to be in charge of the cold case involving the murders of Clementine and Karol Beavers. Mower had been involved early in the investigation back in 1978, but he was not the agent in charge at the time. Larry Goepel had been the lead agent from the beginning of the Beavers' murder investigation. But the BCI had recently transferred Special Agent Goepel to Des Moines to serve as a supervisor. A Vietnam vet, Mower joined the BCI in 1972, directly after his military service. With almost two decades of experience under his belt by 1993, Mower was intimately familiar with murder investigations and had worked a number of cold cases. Before the end of his long career, Special Agent Mower would successfully investigate more than a hundred murder cases. The Beavers' murder investigation would be one of those successes.

In the Beavers' case, Mower began by methodically going back over the entire file, looking for holes, clues, leads, or missed opportunities. This is something he had done before with other investigations and he was skilled at it. He and other investigators soon began re-interviewing witnesses, trying to fill in missing information, to find new evidence. Word quickly spread through the community that the investigation of Monte's involvement in the Beavers' murders was heating back up. Though agents had not yet attempted to interview Monte again, somehow Monte also got word, probably through his brother Donnie, that the heat was being turned up on investigation of his involvement in the Beavers' murders.

Then suddenly out of nowhere in June 1993, Dennis Cornell sent a letter to the *Mount Pleasant News* and to the Henry County Sheriff, claiming he had information about the Beavers' murders. Cornell, one of Monte's few pals from Monte's brief high school days in Mount Pleasant, had his own long history of run-ins with the law. Cornell was first arrested at age 15 for shoplifting and writing bad checks. Through the remainder of his teen years, he had been held in an assortment of juvenile facilities in Quincy, Illinois, Fort Madison, Iowa, and in Mount Pleasant with brief, unsuccessful attempts to reunite him with his family in Mount Pleasant. After committing more crimes, including a burglary where he made off with $6,000, the authorities had enough of trying half-measures with Cornell and incarcerated him in a juvenile facility. In 1978, Cornell was in and out of the boys' home in Eldora, Iowa. Though he escaped once from the facility, he was recaptured and incarcerated there from April 1978 until he was finally released to his parents again on December 1, 1978, about a month after the Beavers had been murdered.

Cornell had gotten himself into a lot more trouble with the law since then. In 1979, Cornell turned 18 years old and soon thereafter was convicted of theft. The judge sentenced Cornell to serve two years in prison. Shortly after being released from prison, Cornell was arrested again in 1981, this time for writing bad checks. Cornell served some more time in prison and then, in 1987, he was convicted of burglary of a business in Burlington, Iowa. But when Cornell failed to appear at his sentencing hearing, the court issued a warrant for his arrest. Eventually, the police tracked him down and Cornell served yet another stint in prison. Then, in 1988, he was convicted of his most serious offense: a robbery-related murder in Morris, Illinois.

Cornell's murder charges arose from the kidnapping and robbery of a stockbroker from Chicago. Cornell had carjacked the man at gunpoint and forced the man to drive to a secluded location. There, Cornell bound the victim's wrists and ankles with duct tape, covered the man's mouth with duct tape, put a plastic bag over his head, and threw him in the trunk of the man's car. The victim slowly suffocated to death. For this wanton act of cruelty, Cornell was convicted of first degree murder and sentenced to 44 years in prison.

By 1993, when Cornell contacted the authorities claiming he had information about the Beavers' murders, he was 32 years old. He wasn't eligible for release from prison until at least 2032.[1] Cornell was serving his time in the Pontiac State Prison in Pontiac, Illinois. That is where the agents went to interview him on July 7, 1993.

Cornell readily agreed to speak with the agents. Before the agents asked Cornell any questions, they advised him of his constitutional rights, as required by the Supreme Court's *Miranda* decision, and Cornell waived those rights. Then, without hesitation or much of a preamble,

---

1. As it turned out, Cornell was paroled out of prison early. Within months of his release, on September 15, 2015, he entered a music store in Davenport, Iowa, and robbed the place, holding a box cutter to the female clerk's neck, using zip ties to bind her hands and feet, and making off with a grand total of $80 from the cash register and $200 cash from her purse. At his trial, Cornell spun a tale that he was actually in a romantic relationship with the victim and the heist was part of an agreement he had with her to pretend he robbed the store because she was having financial difficulties. The jury didn't buy it. The jury convicted Cornell of first-degree robbery and going armed with intent. The court sentenced him to decades in prison.

Cornell bluntly told the agents that he and Monte killed the Beavers. Cornell claimed it was all part of a plan hatched by Max to collect insurance money upon Clementine's death.

According to Cornell, one day he and Monte were out driving around and partying when Monte brought up the subject. Cornell explained that Monte claimed he had a way that they could make a lot of money, but it would have to be something they kept between themselves. Cornell stated that Monte then told him that Max had offered to pay Monte $3,000 to kill Max's wife so Max could collect the life insurance proceeds. Monte offered to pay Cornell half the fee if Cornell helped him commit the murder. Cornell told the agents he agreed to do it.

According to Cornell, on the night of the murders, he and Monte waited in Cornell's car until after midnight. He said they were parked in the parking lot of the Lincoln Elementary School across the street from the Beavers' home. They sat in the car for some time, he explained, trying to work up their nerves. Finally, very early in the morning of October 30, Cornell said he and Monte slipped out of the car and snuck into the Beavers' home through the side door to the garage. Cornell described Monte carrying a .22 caliber rifle, while Cornell said he was armed with a .22 caliber revolver.

Cornell claimed that once they entered the house, he and Monte started rifling through the rooms upstairs to make it look as if a burglary had taken place, as that was part of their alleged plan with Max. Cornell claimed that Monte walked down the hallway on the main floor of the house and peeked into the master bedroom, reporting back to Cornell that Max was asleep in his bed. Then Monte and Cornell headed down to the basement.

Cornell claimed they found both Karol and Clementine asleep in the basement den. Cornell asserted that at this point Monte lost his nerve to commit the murder, so Cornell took the rifle from Monte and just started shooting at Clementine. Cornell claimed he shot at Clementine multiple times and didn't intentionally mean to hit Karol, but did so accidentally. Cornell stated that as he started shooting, Monte ran off. When officers pressed Cornell to provide details about shooting the rifle, Cornell claimed he didn't have to reload the gun and he denied picking up any shell casings.

Cornell explained that after the shooting he quickly left the house and returned to his car still parked in the Lincoln Elementary School parking lot, then he drove home. Cornell stated that at that time he didn't have any idea where Monte had gone to. About an hour and a half later, though, Cornell claimed Monte called him from a pay phone on the square in downtown Mount Pleasant. Cornell told the officers that he drove to the square where he picked up Monte. He said they took Monte's rifle back to Monte's house and threw their clothes in a dumpster behind some store downtown. Then they drove to Gulfport, Illinois where they paid a man to buy them some whiskey. Cornell explained that he and Monte drank for a while before returning to Mount Pleasant later that day. Cornell claimed Monte paid him $1,500 the following day, Cornell's part of the alleged $3,000 fee from Max for killing his wife.

In response to questioning from the officers, Cornell claimed he had dated Karol for a while, but he hadn't seen her for quite some time. Cornell also acknowledged that Monte and he had both been housed in the Burlington jail at the same time for a while. Cornell also claimed that Monte had assured Cornell that he had thoroughly cleaned the rifle so it couldn't be traced back to the murders.

The officers were immediately skeptical of Cornell's story, and for good reason. Although it was true that Clementine had a $17,000 life insurance policy, Cornell's story was inconsistent with many of the known facts, such as how many times Clementine was shot, where Karol was in the home when she was shot, the time of the murders, and so on. Nevertheless, the officers knew they needed to follow up on Cornell's story and it would be a good way to perhaps get Monte to talk with them again.

So, on July 15, 1993, the officers approached Monte while he was still in prison for the Wheelock murder and other crimes and questioned him a third time. After Monte waived his constitutional rights, the agents asked Monte if someone hired him to kill the Beavers. Monte denied it. He asserted that he didn't know anything about Max Beavers until after the murders. Monte acknowledged that he was friends with Cornell, but denied that he was involved with Cornell in killing the Beavers. Special Agent Mower asked Monte if Cornell used his rifle; Monte said that no one used "his rifle." In short, Monte didn't corroborate Cornell's story in any way. But the manner in which he answered Mower's question, Monte at the very least admitted it was his rifle. That would prevent Monte from later claiming the rifle officers seized from his house didn't belong to him.

The agents then pivoted in the interview and began to focus on the particular type of ammunition used to kill Clementine and Karol. The CCI .22 caliber, non-magnum ammunition, the type used to kill the Beavers, wasn't designed for use in Monte's rifle. The agents needed to resolve what could appear to be evidence inconsistent with the idea that Monte's rifle was the murder weapon. Monte readily admitted shooting that type of ammunition with his rifle, though. He explained that the rifle could shoot different types of .22 caliber ammunition, even though the non-magnum shell casings would sometimes jam when trying to discharge a shell casing before loading another round. Monte acknowledged that he bought that ammunition on his father's advice because it was cheaper.

Throughout the interrogation, Monte remained adamant that he had not killed Clementine and Karol.

After questioning Cornell and Monte, Mower took stock of all that he knew of the case at this point and pondered if there was a way to use that information to seek another warrant to seize Monte's rifle. Mower knew that the court had previously suppressed evidence of the rifle and the ballistics testing based on the false affidavit written by Investigator Hagers. But, he reasoned, if he put together all the evidence they had gathered not only during the original investigation but also everything he had dug up in his renewed investigation, then perhaps they could establish probable cause to seize the rifle independent of anything to do with the false assertion that a sheriff allegedly saw Karol's necklace in Monte's house.

On July 26, 1993, fourteen years to the day after execution of the first search warrant, the State obtained and executed a second search warrant to seize the Mossberg rifle. Mower was careful to draft the affidavit in support of the search warrant so as not to rely on any evidence obtained from the prior, unlawful seizure of the firearm. Having reviewed the affidavit, the judge found there was probable cause to believe Monte's rifle was used in the Beavers' murders and authorized Mower to seize the rifle again for use as evidence against Monte. The rifle was still located at the highway patrol office in Mount Pleasant, where it had been stored in evidence since its forfeiture to the state in 1984. Mower didn't have to literally seize it again; rather, the importance of the warrant was that it now authorized the government to use the rifle in evidence. Importantly, it also allowed the government to use the ballistics evidence to show that bullets fired from the weapon matched the bullet fired into Clementine's head.

Having succeeded in seizing the murder weapon again, Special Agent Mower turned to dealing with Cornell's obviously false claim that he and Monte killed the Beavers as part of a plot with Max to collect insurance proceeds. Mower never believed Cornell's version from the start, but he had to confront Cornell about his story and eliminate Cornell's claim as a possible explanation.

On August 13, 1993, Mower and another agent returned to interview Cornell a second time. Again, Cornell waived his *Miranda* rights and agreed to talk with the agents. This time the agents confronted Cornell with facts that showed his version of events was false. They told Cornell that he had a lot of things wrong about the murders.

They told Cornell first of all that records showed he was in the Eldora training school at the time of the murders, so he couldn't possibly have been involved in the murders. Cornell tried to brush that problem aside, insisting that the state records were "all fucked up" and that he was actually living with his parents in Mount Pleasant at the time of the murders.

The agents kept pressing Cornell about the other problems with his story and how it was inconsistent with all the other evidence. And there were lots of problems with his rendition of the facts. The murders didn't occur after midnight. No one had ransacked the house. Clementine wasn't shot multiple times. Karol wasn't shot in the basement. The shell casings were missing. Monte and Cornell wouldn't have needed to pay someone in Gulfport to buy them liquor because, though Cornell was underage at the time, Monte wasn't. And so on.

After being repeatedly confronted with all the false information in his story, Cornell finally admitted he had lied. He explained that not long before he sent the letters to the *Mount Pleasant News* and the sheriff, he and Monte had talked on a three way call arranged through a mutual friend whom Cornell refused to identify. Monte called the friend from prison, who then connected the call with Cornell in a different prison. Cornell admitted that during their conversation, Cornell agreed to "take the swipe" for Monte, meaning he would take responsibility for the murders and in exchange Monte promised to take care of Cornell financially while Cornell served his time in prison.

How Monte would get the money to support him, Cornell never explained. Monte came from a poor family, had been in prison for years, had no job and seemingly no assets. Just how he would allegedly support Cornell financially was unknown.

But the explanation for why Cornell might take the blame for a murder he didn't commit made at least some sense, on the surface. Monte was soon to be released from prison after serving his sentence for the Wheelock murder. On the other hand, Cornell still had a long prison sentence to serve. So, Monte had a lot to gain, and Cornell had little to lose in theory, by Cornell claiming to be the shooter.

Having admitted he lied and explaining why, Cornell then weaved a new story. He insisted that the essence of what he had said before, the story he had told the agents the first time, was still true. Cornell claimed that he was still involved in the murders and that it was still a murder-for-hire situation, and that Karol was still an accidental victim. But, in Cornell's new version of the story, he declared that Monte was the shooter.

In Cornell's revised story, he swore that he stayed outside the house the whole time while Monte was in the Beavers' home alone. He claimed Monte was inside the home for about 20 minutes then came out and they drove away. As they were driving to Gulfport, Cornell said that Monte explained to him how Monte went to the basement and shot Clementine as planned, but that Karol had seen him, so Monte had to kill Karol as well to eliminate her as a witness to Clementine's murder. Cornell claimed, like he did before, that they then took the gun back to Monte's house, ditched their clothes in a dumpster, and headed to Gulfport where they hung out for a while.

The agents remained unconvinced of Cornell's new story. They pointed out to Cornell that Karol was sexually assaulted and that Cornell's version of events failed to explain that key evidence. Cornell then provided a convoluted and confusing explanation that somehow he and Monte split up for some period of time after the murders and before they drove to Gulfport, and it was during that period of about an hour and half, Cornell opined, that Monte must have gone back to the house to rape Karol. The agents continued to confront Cornell about the implausibility of his story, but Cornell kept insisting that his new story was true, even though he admitted lying to the agents before. The agents eventually ended the questioning, convinced that Cornell was once again spinning a tall tale and they were wasting their time talking with him.

Why Cornell falsely confessed to participating in murders he was clearly not involved with remained a mystery. Even if one believed that Monte would support Cornell financially somehow as payment for admitting to committing the murders, Cornell still had a lot to lose. Cornell was not sentenced to prison for life and would be eligible for release eventually. If convicted of killing the Beavers, he would likely receive a life sentence and never be released. Perhaps Cornell thought that by blaming the murder on Max, and cooperating with the state in a prosecution of Max, that Cornell would get a reduced sentence and might even be released early from prison. But that would be taking an extreme risk for only a possible benefit.

It remains hard to image why Cornell would admit to murders he clearly didn't commit. Perhaps one explanation is that Monte had something on Cornell. Perhaps during that three-way call Monte and Cornell had, Monte threatened Cornell with revealing something to the authorities that would get Cornell in even more trouble—perhaps that Cornell was involved in murdering Sue Wheelock—such that Cornell was persuaded to take the blame for the Beavers' murders. If Cornell was convicted of participating in the murder of Sue Wheelock in connection with a burglary, he would be facing life in prison. He wouldn't have any bargaining chips then, like testifying against Max Beavers, that would save him from spending the rest of his life in prison.

In any event, Cornell's versions of how Clementine and Karol were murdered were so clearly absurd that Monte's defense attorneys would never even use it later in Monte's trials to suggest the possibility of reasonable doubt by claiming it was possible that Cornell had murdered them.

Having dispensed with Cornell's false confession, the agents kept working the case against Monte and didn't give up. DNA evidence was first used in a criminal prosecution in the United States in 1987. I know this because as a law student at the time, I published an academic article about it, interviewing the Florida prosecutor who pioneered the use of the new technology in a murder case. So, by the 1990s, through so-called DNA fingerprinting, forensic experts were now able to compare DNA profiles between evidence left at a crime scene and a suspect. In 1994, law enforcement agents attempted to conduct DNA testing of the forensic evidence recovered from the Beavers' murders. The semen recovered from Karol's body was sent for DNA comparison to the blood sample obtained from Monte back in 1979. Unfortunately, sufficient DNA couldn't be detected in the sperm recovered from Karol's body to allow for a valid comparison. The sample had apparently not been adequately preserved for purposes of DNA testing.

Despite the lack of a DNA match, Special Agent Mower became convinced there was still enough evidence to charge Monte with murdering Clementine and Karol Beavers. He approached an Assistant Attorney General, James Kivi, and summarized the evidence he had to prove Monte committed the murders. The two of them then met with Henry County Attorney Mike Riepe, to persuade him that he should file murder charges against Monte. They eventually succeeded in persuading Riepe that there was enough evidence to prove beyond a reasonable doubt that Monte murdered Clementine and Karol.

So, on December 4, 1995, despite lacking definitive DNA evidence, the State of Iowa charged Monte again with two counts of first-degree murder, one count of sexual abuse, and one count of burglary, for the crimes arising from the events of October 29, 1978. Agents traveled to the Anamosa State Penitentiary where Monte was now serving his sentence. At about 8:00 a.m., correctional officers escorted Monte to a meeting room in the prison and when Monte entered the room, the agents served Monte with the Trial Information and Minutes, the formal documents charging him with the Beavers' murders.

The court appointed Dennis Cohen, a state public defender in the Burlington office, to represent Monte.

Then on Monday, December 11, 1995, correctional officers drove Monte from Anamosa to Mount Pleasant and escorted him into a courtroom where, at 11:30 a.m., Monte was arraigned on the charges. The judge tentatively scheduled the trial for April 1996. Bond was set at $1 million, which was academic because Monte was still in custody for the Wheelock murder. About a month later the court appointed Assistant Public Defender John Logan —the attorney who got Monte off the murder charges back in 1984—to join the defense team.

Once again, Monte's defense attorneys dug into the government's evidence and began planning their defense. They took more depositions of potential witnesses and reviewed the new evidence the government had uncovered since 1984. The first line of defense would be, as it was before, an attempt to suppress the evidence and have the case dismissed.

First, Monte's attorneys filed a motion to dismiss the

case alleging the state violated his due process rights by delaying charging him with the crimes for 12 years. Their argument was that the passage of time deprived Monte of his due process rights, reasoning that the passage of time would render the witnesses' testimony so unreliable that Monte couldn't possibly receive a fair trial. The judge rejected that argument out of hand.

Monte's attorneys then filed a motion to once again suppress evidence of the rifle and any fruits of the illegal April 1979 search. The motion also sought to suppress statements made by Monte's brother, Donnie, Monte's father and stepmother, and the recovery of the bullets from the trash dump behind Saunders Park. The defense attorneys argued that the firearm remained tainted evidence because it was seized illegally in 1979 based on Investigator Hagers' false statements. They argued that, but for that illegal search, the police wouldn't have pursued the investigation into the target shooting at the dump, wouldn't have found with Donnie's help the location where they shot at targets, and wouldn't have recovered the bullets that matched the bullet from Clementine's head. The defense attorneys also argued that Monte's father's statements about the type of ammunition Monte used, and his stepmother's statements to officers, were also so-called fruit of the poisonous tree, that is the product of the illegally-seized firearm.

The district court agreed with the defense and granted the defense motion in part. The judge ruled that the rifle itself couldn't be used as evidence because the admissibility of the rifle had already been determined adversely to the

State in the prior case. The district court also suppressed the ballistics testing of the rifle performed after the 1993 seizure, ruling it was a fruit of the illegal 1979 search.

On the other hand, the district court judge denied the defense request to suppress the information gained by the State from its interviews of Monte's stepmother, his father, and his brother since the illegal April 1979 search. The district court held the investigation of Monte as the possible murderer, including whether Monte's .22 caliber Mossberg rifle was the murder weapon, was in progress before the 1979 seizure of the rifle. Because this ongoing investigation, not the 1979 seizure of the rifle, led to interviews of the challenged witnesses and because the 1979 seizure and testing didn't influence the authorities in their questioning of these witnesses, the court concluded that their testimony was untainted by the illegal seizure of the rifle in 1979.

Both sides appealed the district court's ruling to a higher court. While the appeal was pending, the trial was put on hold. The appeal was once again critical. If the appellate court sustained the district court's ruling suppressing the evidence of Monte's firearm and the subsequent ballistics evidence, the government wouldn't have enough evidence to convict Monte of the Beavers' murders. If this evidence was once again suppressed, as it was back in 1980, the State would have to drop the charges again and Monte would once again evade justice for these crimes.

On appeal, the government argued that the court should consider the merits of the later seizure of the firearm in 1993 as if the 1979 search never took place. The government emphasized that the 1993 search warrant did not rely in any way on Hager's false statement or on evidence gained from the illegal seizure of the firearm in 1979. The government's position was that if the 1993 warrant was itself valid, then whether the 1979 warrant existed or not was irrelevant.

The Iowa Supreme Court agreed. The court found that the affidavit Special Agent Mower wrote to support the seizure of Monte's rifle didn't rely in any way on the false information in the 1979 affidavit or on any evidence that came directly from the seizure of the rifle in 1979. Thus, the court reasoned, it was as if the unlawful seizure of the rifle in 1979 never occurred. The government was free to use the rifle and all the ballistic forensic evidence derived from it to prove that Monte was the killer.

The Iowa Supreme Court also affirmed the district court's decision that information gained by the State from its interviews of Monte's father, stepmother, and brother shouldn't be suppressed either. The court agreed with the lower court that the evidence wasn't fruit of the illegal 1979 search because the government was pursuing that evidence regardless of the seizure of the gun from that illegal search. In short, the appeal was a complete win for the government; none of the evidence would be suppressed this time.

The Iowa Supreme Court remanded the case back to the district court with instructions that the district court should allow the case to proceed to trial. Monte's attempt to evade justice failed. The trial was back on. It was 1998, twenty years after the murders.

In the years since Monte murdered Karol and Clementine, the Berlin Wall had fallen and the Soviet Union had dissolved. Personal computers, the internet, and cell phones were developed and transformed daily life. Mount Pleasant had built a new high school on the southeast side of town, converting the old high school Karol had attended into the public library and community center. Clementine's grandchildren had grown to adulthood. And Monte had been in prison.

SEVENTEEN
MONTE ON TRIAL

"Monsters are real. Ghosts are too. They live inside of us, and sometimes, they win." – Stephen King

IN MAY 1998, MONTE WAS PUT ON TRIAL FOR murdering Clementine and Karol. In a strategic move, the government had dropped the sexual assault and burglary charges against Monte. They wanted the focus to be on the murders. And the truth is, if the government couldn't prove Monte guilty of the murders, they couldn't prove him guilty of the two other offenses.

The trial was held in the Henry County Courthouse in Mount Pleasant, an imposing limestone building that, with its grounds, occupies an entire block near the center of town. District Court Judge David Hendrickson presided over the trial. Fondly known by his friends as "D.B.," at age 61, Judge Hendrickson was a no-nonsense, but patient and compassionate judge. He had grown up on a family farm, served in the Army for two years, and earned his law degree with honors from the University of Iowa College of Law the year after Karol Beavers was born. He had become a judge in 1973, just five years before the murders. By 1998, he was a seasoned judge. He lived in Keokuk, a city on the banks of the Mississippi River in Southeast Iowa. It was said of Judge Hendrickson that when he found it difficult to hold his martini while mowing his lawn, he crafted a cup holder for his mower.

The prosecutors were James "Jim" Kivi of the Iowa Attorney General's Office in Des Moines and Henry County Attorney Michael Riepe. The Iowa Attorney General's Office, like the United States Department of Justice, has its own bevy of prosecutors who, among other things, assist county attorneys in prosecuting complex or difficult cases. Titled "Area Prosecutors," these experienced prosecutors, like Kivi, traveled around the state as needed to prosecute cases. Many county prosecutors are over-whelmed, and sometimes ill-equipped, to handle such cases. Assistant Attorney Generals, like Kivi, are highly trained and qualified prosecutors, really the best of the best in the state system.

By 1998, Kivi was an experienced prosecutor, having practiced law since 1975. He grew up in a Chicago suburb. Kivi was drafted into the Army shortly after he graduated from college and was sent to Vietnam. Kivi actually took the LSAT—the admission test for law school —while serving in Vietnam. After his military service, he attended and graduated from the University of Iowa

College of Law. For a few years, he practiced law in a firm in a small town in Iowa before joining the Attorney General's office as an Area Prosecutor in 1980. By the time he prosecuted the Beavers' murders, Kivi had prosecuted at least a dozen other murder cases. Riepe, the elected Henry County Attorney, by comparison, had only tried a couple murder cases before the Seager trial in 1998. Kivi naturally took the lead in the prosecution.

The Seager trial would be a difficult case for the government to win. In criminal cases, prosecutors must prove each element of an offense by proof beyond a reasonable doubt. That is the highest burden of proof in the law. The burden of "proof beyond a reasonable doubt" isn't amenable to an easy definition. In civil cases, parties typically have a burden of proof called preponderance of the evidence. That simply means that it's more likely true than not true. Anything over 50%, and the party has carried its burden. So, proof beyond a reasonable doubt is certainly higher than 50%, but the law doesn't assign it a percentage. It means something greater than thinking the defendant likely committed the crime, or even that the defendant probably did it. Various courts have crafted an assortment of words in an attempt to define proof beyond a reasonable doubt. Some judges instruct juries that proof beyond a reasonable doubt means "proof that leaves you firmly convinced of the defendant's guilt, but is not proof beyond all doubt." Whatever the definition, it is made clear to jurors that proof beyond a reasonable doubt is a very high standard indeed.

To overcome the very high burden of proof, the

government had relatively little to work with. There was no direct evidence linking Monte to the murders. Direct evidence consists of testimony by witnesses based on their own observations, or on physical evidence directly linking an offender to a crime scene. Rather, the government's evidence was largely based on circumstantial evidence. Circumstantial evidence depends on logic. Circumstantial evidence are facts that point toward guilt through a chain of circumstances that leads to a logical conclusion. An example often used by lawyers to explain to jurors the difference between direct and circumstantial evidence is snowfall. If a witness testifies to seeing it snow, or there is a video of it snowing, that is direct evidence that it snowed. If a witness testifies that she went to bed one night and there was no snow on the ground, but that there was snow on the ground the next day when she woke up, that is circumstantial evidence that it snowed. By 1998, the law made no distinction between direct and circumstantial evidence. Jurors were allowed to afford evidence of either kind whatever weight they thought appropriate.

In the Beavers' case, there was no direct testimonial evidence Monte killed Clementine or Karol. No witness saw Monte murder the Beavers. Indeed, no witness saw Monte anywhere near the Beavers' home—ever. There was no evidence that, before the murder, Monte even knew where Karol lived. There was no evidence Monte ever threatened Karol or expressed any desire to ever harm her. There was no evidence Karol ever spurned Monte or did anything else to give rise to a motive for Monte to harm her. And Monte had never made an incriminating statement about the murders to anyone, including the police during multiple interviews. No witness would be able to testify that they had any first-hand knowledge of any kind that Monte murdered Karol and Clementine. And, to the contrary, there was some evidence from Monte's stepmother that corroborated his alibi that he was at home watching television the evening when Karol and Clementine were slaughtered.

As far as direct physical evidence against Monte, it was weak. The strongest forensic evidence the government had was ballistics testing that showed markings—scars, if you will—left on bullets shot from Monte's rifle matched markings left on a single bullet recovered from Clementine's head. That testing was subject to attack, of course, because it was based on mere human eyesight comparison and opinion. Further, the ballistics evidence couldn't establish who pulled the trigger; it could, at best, only tie Monte's gun to the murders. Others, like Monte's brother Donnie, did or may have had access to the weapon as well.

The only other physical evidence that could possibly link Monte to the crime scene was blood—the killer and rapist was a Type O secreter, as was Monte. But, so, too, was about 35% of the population. The government had no fingerprints, no hair samples, no other forensic evidence linking Monte to the scene. To the contrary, that type of forensic evidence pointed to another, unknown killer. A fingerprint left on the car next to Karol's body didn't come back to match Monte, or anyone else for that matter. The same was true of a lone pubic hair found on Karol's jeans; it certainly didn't match Monte and the government had no idea whose pubic hair it was. The defense attorneys would have a field day with this conflicting and weak evidence.

Monte was represented by public defenders. Assistant Public Defender John Logan continued to represent Monte. Another Assistant Public Defender, Tyler Johnston, had replaced Dennis Cohen while Monte's case had been on appeal. Both Logan and Johnston were experienced criminal defense attorneys from Cedar Rapids. Logan was the more senior attorney with several decades' experience and he had been involved representing Monte now for decades. But even the younger and less experienced attorney, Johnston, had been practicing law for 13 years by the time of trial. Both attorneys were skilled and knew how to exploit the weaknesses in the government's evidence. They could be counted upon to do so to the best of their abilities.

*Henry County Courthouse, Mount Pleasant, Iowa
(photo by author)*

Monte's attorneys tried to have the venue—the location—of the trial changed from Mount Pleasant. Generally, a trial is held in the county where the crime occurred, in this case Henry County. If there is too much adverse publicity, a criminal defendant can ask the court to move the trial to another county where, presumably, there isn't so much publicity. The concern, of course, is that the jurors are pulled from the county where the case is prosecuted. If a case is of such a notorious nature that adverse publicity pervades the local area, it may be difficult to seat a jury of impartial jurors not already adversely impacted by the bad publicity. To such jurors, Monte may already have been convicted in the court of public opinion.

In moving for a change of venue, Monte's attorneys

argued that there was no way Monte could receive a fair trial in Mount Pleasant because of all the adverse publicity about him and the case in the local news. The defense attorneys had hired some people to conduct a random poll of the local population to prove they were already unfairly biased against Monte and couldn't be fair jurors. The polling of citizens in the area showed, as predicted, a lot of people knew about the Beavers' murders and many of them had already reached conclusions about Monte's guilt based on what they had heard or read in the news.

Judge Hendrickson held an evidentiary hearing on this defense motion, during which he considered the defense polling evidence and heard argument from the attorneys. In the end the court denied the defense motion for a change of venue. The court found that the adverse publicity had not so thoroughly pervaded the public that every prospective juror was bound to have heard of the case or have an opinion, especially given the age of much of the publicity. The murders had taken place two decades before. Since that time, there had been little in the news about the murders or about Monte Seager. Judge Hendrickson was also confident that, through the jury selection process itself, the court could remove those prospective jurors who had made up their minds already based on publicity.

Jury selection began on May 19, 1998, and it took two days. More than 60 prospective jurors were summoned. The potential jurors were questioned at length, both individually and as a group, by attorneys for both sides. Much of the questioning was focused on whether the prospective juror knew anything or had heard anything about the case or about Monte Seager and, if so, whether they had formed an opinion about his guilt. The judge granted defense motions to strike for cause several prospective jurors who opined that they had heard about the case and had already concluded Monte was guilty. But many of the prospective jurors knew nothing about the case and had formed no opinions. Some of the prospective jurors had tangential connections to law enforcement officers, but not significant enough of a connection to cause them to be struck from the jury.

At the conclusion of the questioning, Monte's attorneys renewed their motion for a change of venue, arguing that Monte could not receive a fair trial. The government resisted the motion and the judge denied it. Judge Hendrickson found that the jury selection proccss was sufficient to remove tainted jurors. He then had the attorneys exercise their peremptory strikes, where each side is allowed to remove a number of prospective jurors from the panel so as to reduce the number down to the 12 needed to decide Monte's fate. The jury ultimately selected to decide the case consisted of nine women and three men.

The trial lasted nine days. Throughout the trial, Monte made handwritten notes in a notebook. His attorneys gave him the notebook to use as it is often best for criminal defendants to have something to do during a trial, especially something that keeps their heads down, so that jurors don't read something into the defendants' expressions, or lack of expressions, as witnesses testify.

In this case, Monte's attorneys gave him the notebook

the first time they met with him soon after he was charged. So, Monte actually began taking notes in 1995. By the end of the trial, Monte's notes filled a 79-page notebook and, after he filled every line on every page on one side, he turned the notebook over and started writing on the back sides of the pages for another 17 pages. Monte wrote his notes in a very neat, precise, cursive hand. He carefully dated each entry, much as in the form of a diary. But the notebook didn't mention any personal information; it only addressed his legal proceedings from the initial charges through trial, including notes he made of conversations he had with his attorneys, observations he made while attending pretrial depositions of witnesses, and his observations made during his trial.

Monte's notes also included occasional observations from his transport to and from court proceedings from prison. One time in February 1995, he noted that it was -23 degrees outside as he rode in a jail van from prison to court at 5:30 a.m. He observed that there were many semitrucks broken down along the roadside. On another occasion in the spring of 1995, he noted that there were "a lot of dandylions [sic] along the road." In another entry about a trip to court on March 1, 1998, Monte noted "weather overcast with light snow. Saw one patch of blue sky."

His notes about the legal proceedings themselves were very thorough and detailed. He took down some testimony given at trial almost verbatim. The notes also reflected Monte clearly understood the legal maneuvers of his attorneys and the court rulings. At one point, it even mentions him recommending his attorneys read a particular book on forensic ballistics.

At another point in his notes, it reveals details of and his thoughts about plea negotiations. His attorneys told Monte about some preliminary plea discussions they had with the prosecutors and hypothesized that perhaps they could negotiate a plea to second degree murder with a 25-year sentence. Monte wrote: "I told them I wasn't interested."

During jury selection, Monte expressed in his notes concerns about whether jurors might be biased against him because some of them had indirect connections to law enforcement officers. He wrote: "Hope is all that I have. Please GOD free me from the oppression of the wicked. Hope in GOD."

Monte Seager appearing for trial 1998 (photo by
Mount Pleasant News)

During the trial itself, Monte steadily took notes in his notebook. The Beavers family noticed him feverishly taking notes and often wondered what he was writing in them. Many years later, a granddaughter of Clementine and cousin of Karol wrote a letter to Monte in jail, asking him about the notes and what he wrote. Monte responded by sending the notebook to that relative. Years after that, she sent the notebook to me as part of my research for this book.

As Monte took his notes, the government began the trial with its opening statement. The government's opening was plain and straightforward. The prosecutor laid out the basic details of the Beavers' murders. He marched through the forensic evidence recovered at the scene and the testing that was done. He told about the evidence that would show when, where, and how Monte bought the .22 caliber rifle, and how forensic testing showed that the markings on the bullet recovered from Clementine's head matched the lands and grooves of the rifling in the barrel of Monte's rifle. He described the results of Karol's autopsy, the fact the secreter of the semen and saliva recovered from Karol's body came from someone with Type O blood, who was a secreter, and that Monte was a Type O blood secreter. As prosecution opening statements go, it was methodical, thorough, and workman-like.

The defense opening statement was less methodical and more aggressive. The defense made it clear from the beginning that its theme was that the police conducted an inadequate investigation, made assumptions, and jumped to conclusions. The defense asserted from the start that the case against Monte was based on rumors, assumptions, and speculation. "Whoever committed those two crimes is a monster," the defense bluntly conceded, but boldly proclaimed that Monte was not that monster, that he was "innocent of these two murders."

The defense opening statement focused primarily on two pieces of evidence. The first was the forensic evidence from the scene, in particular the lone pubic hair found on Karol's jeans. The defense attorney argued that the pubic hair must have come from the rapist, but it didn't match Monte. The defense attorney also pointed out that the fingerprints officers found on the car near where Karol was raped and died didn't come back to Monte either, and, more important, had not been matched to anyone.

The other focus by the defense attorney during the opening statement was on Monte's alibi. Given the timing of when Max went to bed, Clementine's unfailing routine of going to bed and locking up the house at 10:00 p.m., and the evidence from the autopsy approximating the time of death, the defense pointed out that the evidence would show that the murders must have occurred between 8:00 and 10:00 p.m. The defense attorney emphasized that the evidence would show that Monte was at home watching TV during that window of time. The attorney pointed out that Monte recited details from the same TV show that Investigator Hagers had watched, showing that Monte had clearly stayed home and watched the entire movie. The defense explained that Monte could not have left his house after the movie to commit the murders because he answered the telephone at 10:00 p.m. when his stepmother's mother called. The defense further pointed out that Monte's stepmother saw him still in the house when she left for work a little after 10:30 p.m. And, the murders occurred before 10:00 p.m. anyway, so where Monte was after 10:00 would be irrelevant.

After the lawyers completed opening statements, the government began putting on its evidence. The government began its case by calling elderly Max Beavers, the husband and father of the victims, to the stand. Through careful and methodical questioning, Max Beavers recounted the events of the day before and the night of the murders, and his awful discovery of his slain family. The defense cross examination hinted at Max having a motive to kill his wife, but mostly focused on what he didn't know, didn't see, couldn't answer, because he was asleep.

Sergeant Terry Duncan, the first officer at the scene, testified next. He told about responding to the emergency call, what happened, what he saw, and what he did when he arrived at the scene. Sergeant Duncan later recalled looking over at Monte while he testified in the trial. "I had dealt with a lot of murder cases since the Beavers' murders," he later told me, "but I had never seen anyone with such cold eyes as those I saw in Monte Seager the day I testified." With Sergeant Duncan, as with the other law enforcement officers, the defense attorney's cross examination focused on holes in the investigation, things the officers could have done, but didn't, to better preserve the crime scene, uncover evidence, or avoid tainting evidence at the scene.

The government then called numerous officers and other witnesses to recount the recovery of the victims' bodies and discovery of evidence at the scene, to repeat the statements Monte made to investigators during interviews, and to testify about how the investigators eliminated other suspects through their investigation. The government also called the Coast-to-Coast salesman to testify about selling the rifle to Monte and about the ammunition used in the weapon. The prosecutors read into evidence the deposition testimony of Harry Seager and Sharon Gaylord because they had both passed away by the time of the trial.

At one point in the trial, the government tried to call Donnie Seager to testify. But Donnie refused. Donnie was himself in custody at the time, serving one of his own prison sentences. Donnie had been convicted of armed robbery in 1982, escape in 1987, and later of engaging in lascivious acts with a child. When the prosecutor announced Donnie Seager as the government's next witness, a deputy sheriff escorted Donnie into the courtroom.

When Donnie took the stand to testify, however, he quickly became belligerent and combative. At first, he answered a few innocuous questions about who he was in relation to Monte and where he was living back in 1978. But when Prosecutor Kivi asked Donnie if Monte owned a gun, Donnie refused to answer the question. Judge Hendrickson ordered Donnie to answer. Donnie refused again, glaring at the judge. When the judge threatened to hold him in contempt, Donnie told the judge what he could do with his threat of contempt. The Beavers family, watching the proceeding from the gallery of the court-room, found Donnie very frightening.

Donnie's defiant reaction surprised Kivi. The prose-

cutor had met with Donnie before trial to review his antic-
ipated testimony, as any careful prosecutor would do, and
nothing in that prep session had provided a clue that
Donnie would explode, or implode, when he hit the
witness stand. Sitting directly across from Monte, looking
his brother in the eye, must have been too much for
Donnie for him to go through with his testimony. After
Donnie refused to testify and Judge Hendrickson
dismissed him from the courtroom, the judge permitted
the government to read into evidence the testimony
Donnie gave during a deposition instead. Although this
was not as good as live testimony might be, it got into
evidence the key information the prosecution needed
about Donnie and Monte shooting the rifle at targets near
Saunders Park.

The main focus of the government's evidence presentation was scientific, however, emphasizing the results of the
autopsies, the ballistics testing matching Monte's gun to
the murder, and Monte's O positive blood type connected
with the bodily fluids he left in and on Karol. This was
also the focus of the defense attorneys' most vigorous cross
examination. Their questions focused on the timing of the
murders, and how long Karol may have laid in the kitchen
before the killer dragged her body into the garage, so as to
build the case for Monte's alibi that he was at home when
the murders occurred. The defense attorneys also focused
their questioning, of course, on the forensic evidence
found at the scene—the pubic hair and blond hair found
on Karol's body, and the fingerprints on the family car
parked near her body—that didn't match Monte.

During the trial, the government offered evidence, almost as an aside, that Monte was involved in growing marijuana. It came up simply in the context of explaining Monte's inconsistent explanations he gave to officers about where he was the night of the murders. In his first interview, given days after the murders, Monte claimed he never left the house the night of the murders. That was inconsistent with his father's recollection of hearing Monte leave the house after Sharon, his common law wife, left for work. When, many years later, officers interviewed him once again, this time in prison, they confronted him with this inconsistency. This time, Monte admitted that on the night of the murders he stepped outside of his house twice, but he said it was only to water his marijuana plants. That statement was inconsistent with his prior denial of leaving the house at all, which he made during his first interview. The reference to the marijuana wasn't important to the murder case. The inconsistencies of his stories, however, was at least some indication of Monte's guilt. The government wanted to emphasize the inconsistent stories and, in explaining his inconsistent stories, repeated Monte's claim that he stepped outside the house a couple times the night of the murders to water his marijuana plants. The defense objected to admission of testimony referencing Monte growing marijuana on the basis that it would be prejudicial to Monte, but the judge overruled the objection.

The government rested its case on Wednesday, May 27, 1998, just a few minutes after noon.

The judge turned to defense counsel and asked if they

wished to present evidence on behalf of the defendant. Logan stood up and said they did not, and that the defense rested.

The defense didn't call any witnesses on Monte's behalf. And they didn't call Monte himself to testify. Monte's attorneys had explained to him before trial that it would be against his best interest to testify. As it stood, the jury never heard any evidence that Monte had been convicted of murdering Sue Wheelock, or about any of the other crimes he committed in connection with Sue's murder or his subsequent escape. Such evidence would have been deemed too unfairly prejudicial. Labeled "propensity evidence," the fear is that such evidence of an unrelated crime would lead jurors to convict Monte on the ground that if he murdered one person, he must have also murdered the Beavers. That is, that Monte just had the propensity to kill people. Justice demands that jurors make decisions based on the evidence and not on presumptions that people act consistent with some predisposition. Monte's attorneys had filed a motion with the court before trial to keep out evidence of Monte's other murder, which the court granted.

So, the jurors who would decide Monte's fate would be completely in the dark about him having murdered Sue Wheelock, having escaped from a jail, having burglarized multiple homes and businesses, and were even unaware that he was serving a sentence in prison at the time of trial. On the other hand, Monte's attorneys explained to him, if Monte took the stand then it would make his credibility directly at issue. Under the rules of evidence, the prosecutors could then cross examine Monte and bring out his prior felony convictions, not to show propensity—that is, not to argue that because he killed Sue Wheelock he must have killed Clementine and Karol Beavers—but, rather, to show that as a convicted felon the jurors should not believe his testimony. In short, as Monte's attorneys explained, if Monte stayed off the stand, the jury would never know that he was a convicted murderer. On the other hand, if he testified, it would all come out. Monte would be a fool to testify under these circumstances. And Monte was no fool. So he never testified and the jury never knew about all the other crimes he had committed.

Once both sides rested their cases, the judge excused the jury until the following day. Then, outside the presence of the jury, Judge Hendrickson took up with the attorneys the issue of jury instructions. At the end of a trial, before the jury deliberates, judges read instructions to the jury informing them of what the law is and giving them direction about how to conduct their deliberations. In Monte's trial, the question arose whether the judge should instruct the jury on a lesser-included offense of second degree murder.

To prove first degree murder, the state would have to show Monte killed Clementine and/or Karol "willfully, deliberately, and with premeditation" or killed them while participating in a forceable felony. A forceable felony includes burglary, but there was no evidence Monte entered the Beavers' residence to burglarize it. A forceable felony also includes sexual abuse, however. Whoever killed Karol sexually abused her. There could have been some question about whether the killing was committed "while participating in" the sexual abuse or whether he killed her and then decided to sexually abuse her body. The fact that she was still bleeding when raped, which suggested she was still alive when raped, was important to that issue. To avoid these unnecessary complications, the prosecution was pushing the theory that Monte acted willfully, deliberately, and with premeditation, and did not pin their argument on showing that he committed the murders while participating in a forceable felony. Murder in the first degree in Iowa is punishable by mandatory life in prison without parole.

Under Iowa law, murder in the second degree is a "lesser-included" offense of first degree murder. Second degree murder occurs when a "person commits murder which is not murder in the first degree." To prove second degree murder, the government need only prove a killing with malice aforethought. Malice aforethought requires the killer to have a fixed purpose or design to do physical harm to another that exists before the act is committed. Proving second degree murder is much easier than proving first degree murder. For Monte to be guilty of second degree murder, the state would not have to prove he acted with premeditation or that he committed murder in commission of a forceable felony. In Iowa in 1998, murder in the second degree was punishable by a mandatory minimum sentence of ten years and up to life in prison.

Thus, each side had some motivation to have the jury consider murder in the second degree as an option. The lesser-included offense option could serve a sort of safety net function for the government to prevent Monte from being set free. In other words, if the jury struggled in deciding whether Monte committed first degree murder, at least the government could walk away with a second degree murder conviction. This is the outcome the government willingly negotiated with Monte in a plea deal over his murder of Sue Wheelock. If the jury convicted Monte of murder in the second degree, the government could always still ask for a life sentence, even though it wouldn't be a mandatory sentence.

For Monte and his defense attorneys, there was a clear motivation for him to have the jury consider murder in the second degree. If convicted of first degree murder, Monte would never be a free man. If convicted of second degree murder, there was a chance his attorneys could persuade the judge to impose a sentence of less than life in prison. Monte wasn't yet 40 years old. Even if Judge Hendrickson imposed a lengthy 25- or 30-year sentence, there would still be a chance Monte could leave prison before he died. Plus, Monte would be eligible for parole at some point, which would not be an option if the jury convicted him of first degree murder.

Judges will almost always instruct juries about lesser-included offenses and allow the juries to consider that option if either side requests the instruction and there is any evidence that would support a lesser-included offense conviction. Somewhat surprisingly here, neither side asked Judge Hendrickson to do so. To the contrary, both the government and Monte's attorneys asked Judge Hendrickson to only instruct the jury on first degree murder. In other words, both sides decided to gamble. It would be all or nothing. Monte would either be found guilty of first degree murder and never be a free man, or would be found not guilty and walk free.

For the government, this reflected confidence in the strength of its case. A lesser-included-offense instruction is more attractive to prosecutors when they recognize that their case is weak. Here, the prosecutors felt sufficiently confident in their case that they didn't see a need for a safety net. But it was a risk. The evidence of Monte's guilt was anything but overwhelming.

Monte and his attorneys' decision to forgo an instruction on the lesser-included offense of second degree murder may have reflected a realistic assessment of the sentence he would receive even if he was found guilty of the lesser-included offense. In May 1976, the Iowa Supreme Court affirmed a sentence of life in prison for a defendant who killed a gas station attendant in an attempted robbery.[1] Monte's attorneys were likely familiar with this case, and others like it, where judges sentenced offenders to life in prison despite a conviction for a lesser-included offense of murder in the second degree. Monte and his attorneys must have recognized that the facts in that 1976 case were far less egregious than those present in the Beavers' murders. Plus, Monte had already been convicted of another murder. Monte and his attorneys may very well have concluded that Judge Hendrickson would sentence him to life in prison without parole even if

1. *State v. Smith*, 242 N.W.2d 320 (Iowa 1976).

the jury came back with a second degree murder verdict. That wasn't an unreasonable prediction. If a life sentence was the likely outcome of being found guilty of murder in the second degree, then it made sense to gamble on the jury acquitting Monte outright.

In any event, with both sides agreeing that the jury should only be instructed on the elements of first degree murder, Judge Hendrickson drafted the instructions and jury verdict form accordingly. The jury would have only two options: guilty of first degree murder or not guilty. If the jury convicted Monte, Judge Hendrickson would be bound to sentence Monte to life in prison without parole. If the jury acquitted Monte of first degree murder, he would walk free. The stakes were as high as they could get in a state that had abolished the death penalty in 1965.

The following day, the attorneys presented their closing arguments to the jury. The government's closing argument marched methodically through the evidence presented at trial. Like its opening statement, the government's closing argument focused on the forensic evidence, particularly the blood type and ballistics. The prosecutor made no attempt to identify a motive for the murders. Indeed, the prosecutor conceded the government couldn't establish a motive, but emphasized that the government didn't have to supply one. "Why did the defendant shoot Clementine and Karol?" Prosecutor Kivi asked rhetorically. "We don't know. We don't have to prove it. There is no logic in crime."

Throughout the trial, Monte had shown no emotion. When the prosecutors displayed horrifying photos of

Karol and Clementine's bodies, Monte had no reaction. He sat there impassively. The temptation must have been great for Kivi to comment during closing argument on Monte's lack of natural human emotions, but he could not. Monte did not testify, and therefore his reaction or lack of reaction were not available for comment because they were not in evidence. The Beavers family members who sat through the trial and watched Monte noted Monte's lack of response; surely, the jurors did, too, without Kivi having to point it out.

During the defense closing argument, the defense attorneys maintained the theme with which the defense started the trial. The defense team each gave part of the closing argument. Attorney Logan began: "A monstrous act was committed in the community 20 years ago," the defense attorney conceded, but it wasn't Monte who was the monster, he insisted. The defense attorney then moved on to attack the sloppiness of the investigation, pointing out several mistakes and omissions in the recording of evidence and the like. More importantly, the defense pushed the idea that the killer used a revolver, not a rifle. The defense attorney emphasized that the absence of shell casings showed the killer used a handgun, specifically a revolver. The defense attorney also pointed out that the first shot to Karol, the one that passed through her arm and her cheek, wouldn't have incapacitated her, as the government's evidence showed. So, the defense attorney reasoned, Karol would have been able to run away and scream for help after being shot the first time unless she was shot again very quickly. The fact that she didn't run and scream means, the defense attorney reasoned, that the killer had to have shot her the second time very quickly after the first shot, an act he could accomplish only with a handgun. Had the killer used a rifle, the defense attorney argued, it would have taken too long to reload and Karol would have run away, screaming for help, awakening her father. It was a clever argument.

During his portion of the closing argument, Defense Attorney Johnston focused again on the forensic evidence from the crime scene that didn't match up to Monte Seager. He reminded the jury of the lone pubic hair found on Karol's jeans that was not hers, and was not Monte's, and could only have belonged to the real rapist and killer. He also reminded the jury of the fingerprints left on the family Buick next to Karol's body, the prints that didn't match Monte Seager and prints that the police had failed to link to the real killer. And he reminded the jury of Monte's alibi—that Monte was watching a movie at the time of the murders—an alibi corroborated by Investigator Hagers who had seen the same movie.

Attorney Johnston ended the closing argument for the defense by returning to the theme that the government's case was based on assumptions and rumors.

"I have sympathy for the Beavers, for this case. It does not help them that the wrong person is convicted. Let's stop this now, the rumors, the speculation. Maybe the killer is dead, in jail, who knows where. If you convict Monte, the real killer will sit back and laugh."

In the government's rebuttal closing argument, Prosecutor Kivi minimized the significance of any errors made by law enforcement officers in conducting the investigation, arguing that they had no impact on the reliability of the evidence. Turning to address the defense argument that the killer used a revolver, the prosecutor pointed out that the first shot to Karol's arm and face was more than a glancing blow. The prosecutor explained that the shot to her cheek fractured her cheekbone. He argued that the first shot was an amply serious injury to at least stun Karol and knock her to the ground, long enough for Monte to reload his rifle and shoot her again.

The lawyers finished their arguments a little after the noon hour. After Judge Hendrickson read the jury instructions to the jury, the case was submitted to the jurors for their deliberations around 2:00 p.m. on Thursday, May 28. While the jurors deliberated in the jury room, everyone else waited for the jury to return with a verdict. Monte wrote in his journal: "In God I hope for Not Guilty. A prayer of hope to God."

By 5:00 p.m., the jury had still not reached a verdict, so the judge sent the jurors home for the night with instructions to return the following morning to continue their deliberations.

The morning of Friday, May 29, 1998, began with an overcast sky and a light drizzle. The jury renewed their deliberations at 9:00 a.m. As with every other day of trial, the Beavers family began the day in a room set aside for them in the courthouse, reciting the Lord's Prayer. Then they waited for a jury decision. A short time later, around 10:00 a.m., the Beavers family received word that the jury had reached a unanimous verdict.

Judge Hendrickson gathered everyone back into the courtroom. Deputies brought Monte into the courtroom and escorted him to a seat between his two defense attorneys. When everyone was assembled and ready, the judge instructed the bailiff to usher the jury into the jury box.

The jurors shuffled into the courtroom, none of them looking directly at Monte. The foreperson of the jury handed the verdict form to the bailiff, who passed it on to the judge. After he perused the verdict form for a moment, Judge Hendrickson pronounced the jury's verdict: guilty of murder in the first degree of Clementine Beavers; guilty of murder in the first degree of Karol Beavers.

Monte sat impassively as the judge announced the verdict. He wrote in his notebook: "I don't believe it."

Judge Hendrickson thanked the jurors for their service, then excused them from the courtroom. The judge then announced that the sentencing hearing would take place a month later, on June 30, 1998, at 1:00 p.m. Then he adjourned court.

The Beavers family was elated by the verdict. It had been 20 long years. In that time, Max had remarried, and ultimately moved into a different house with his new wife. Every year on the anniversary of Clementine and Karol's murders, the family met with their priest in remembrance of their dearly departed loved ones. During these years, the family watched the criminal justice system grind slowly on, saw Monte charged with the murders and then saw the criminal justice system throw out the evidence against him and were despondent when the state dropped the charges.

The family members felt the renewed hope when Special Agent Mower reinvigorated the investigation and when Monte was again charged, but suffered the pangs of memory as the family members were forced to relive the awful events and witness the evidence during the trial. But now, at long last, it was over. Monte had been convicted. Justice had been achieved.

On June 30, 1998, Monte appeared again at the Henry County Courthouse before Judge Hendrickson to be sentenced for his monstrous crimes. At the sentencing hearing, Judge Hendrickson accepted victim impact statements submitted by members of the Beavers family. One family member, a niece, asked and was allowed to read her statement out loud in the courtroom. Judge Hendrickson listened to the arguments of counsel, but the arguments were largely pro forma because the mandatory sentence of life without parole was dictated by the statute and a foregone conclusion. Judge Hendrickson also gave Monte an opportunity to make a statement, but Monte declined to say a word. Judge Hendrickson then imposed two consecutive life sentences. Again, as he did throughout the trial, Monte showed no emotion when Judge Hendrickson told him he would die in prison.

EIGHTEEN

THE APPEAL

"The liberties of none are safe unless the liberties of all are protected." – Supreme Court Justice William O. Douglas

BUT, IT TURNED OUT, THE STORY WASN'T OVER YET. Monte's attorneys swiftly appealed his conviction. On November 4, 1999, the Iowa Court of Appeals heard oral argument by the lawyers. Many members of the Beavers family drove to Des Moines to attend the oral argument.

A few months later after the oral argument, in an unpublished decision, the Iowa Court of Appeals reversed Monte's conviction and granted him a new trial. The court found that Judge Hendrickson shouldn't have allowed the government to admit evidence about Monte growing marijuana. The appellate court concluded the reference to Monte's marijuana grow was too unrelated to the murder investigation to be relevant to any issue before the jury and was therefore unfairly prejudicial to Monte. The court held that Monte was deprived of a fair trial by reference to the marijuana. So, it reversed his conviction and remanded the case for a new trial.[1] The government sought further review from the Iowa Supreme Court, but it was turned down. Once again, Monte evaded justice.

The Court of Appeals' decision was an unexpected shock to the prosecution and the Beavers family. From an evidentiary standpoint, there was ample reason for the trial court to have found that the fact Monte changed his story about leaving the house the night of the murders was admissible evidence. For obvious reasons, leaving the house the night of the murders, versus staying home all night, provided some evidence that Monte had the opportunity to commit the murders. Plus, his shifting story was itself some evidence of guilt. That Monte claimed to leave the house to water his marijuana plants was all just part of his false story. Indeed, the government wasn't trying to prove that Monte actually had marijuana plants and that he left the house to water them; to the contrary, the government wanted the jury to recognize it was a false story and to believe that Monte left the house to commit the murders.

There was a very strong basis, then, for Judge Hendrickson to find the evidence relevant to the proceedings. On appeal, Monte's attorneys didn't disagree. Rather, their argument on appeal was that the reference to Monte's

---

1. *State v. Seager*, No. 98-1195, 199 WL 1072666 (Iowa App. Nov. 23, 1999).

marijuana grow was of marginal evidentiary value but was highly prejudicial to Monte. The Court of Appeals agreed, and found that any reference to narcotics usage was so highly prejudicial that it required reversal.

Trial judges' difficult evidentiary rulings are typically granted a large degree of deference by appellate courts. After all, the trial judge is there on the scene, more fully familiar with the facts, and is in a much better position to make a difficult balancing decision about the admissibility of evidence than appellate judges reviewing a cold record on paper. For that reason, few convictions are overturned based on debatable evidentiary rulings. But this conviction was.

It was also stunning that the Court of Appeals believed the passing reference to marijuana plants deprived Monte of a fair trial. Even when trial judges make erroneous evidentiary rulings, that does not necessarily require a reversal of a conviction. If a court determines that evidence was admitted erroneously, the question then becomes whether the evidence was so prejudicial to the defendant that there would be a miscarriage of justice were he not granted a new trial. Or, put the other way, the question becomes whether the error was harmless. An appellate court must decide whether the erroneously admitted error of such a minor nature, compared with all the other evidence, would have made no material differ-ence in the outcome of the case.

Monte was on trial for a double homicide and the brutal rape of a sixteen-year-old girl as she lay dying on a cold garage floor. He stood accused of the premeditated, cold blooded murder of a 58 year old woman who was innocently watching TV. The idea, the thought, that a mere mention that he told investigators he allegedly watered marijuana plants would cause a jury to convict an otherwise innocent man strains credulity. One would have to believe that the jurors would have otherwise acquitted Monte except the jurors were so incensed that he was a pothead that they convicted him of a crime he didn't commit. It is inconceivable that the jurors gave a second thought to whether Monte smoked or even distributed marijuana. What juror could possibly care about marijuana under these circumstances? The focus of the trial was on his brutal murders; the marijuana was a passing reference.

Yet, the Iowa Court of Appeals thought otherwise. The Court of Appeals' judges were of the opinion that the evidence against Monte wasn't so overwhelming as to find admission of the marijuana evidence harmless error. In its written opinion, the Court of Appeals did not specifically address the nature of the case and the evidence. The strength of the evidence is only one part of a harmless error analysis. A court must also consider the nature of the case, the evidence, and what impact the allegedly prejudicial evidence could have on the deliberations given the nature of all the other evidence in the case. It isn't enough to simply say the questioned evidence is highly prejudicial and that the other evidence of guilt isn't overwhelming. Nevertheless, the Court of Appeals didn't engage in this analysis, at least in writing. Its harmless error analysis consisted of a single sentence: "We, like the court in *Liggins* [referring to another case involving circumstantial evidence], do not find the earlier recited evidence against Seager so overwhelming that it supports a finding of harmless error."

So there it was. Monte's conviction was overturned and the case remanded for a new trial. The consequences of the Court of Appeals' reversal was significant. It wasn't simply that the state would have to retry Monte. Before it could do so, Monte might be set free.

By the time the Court of Appeals rendered its decision, in February 2000, Monte had nearly completed serving his 50-year sentence for the charges arising from the Wheelock murder. He had repeatedly been denied parole, but in the state system inmates don't actually serve every day of a sentence imposed. Rather, prisoners earn a day or two of credit for every day served, such that someone sentenced to 50 years in prison may only actually serve about half that time, or less. So, by now Monte was about to be set free.

To prevent Monte from being released from custody, the government quickly filed a motion asking the court to order that Monte be held in custody pending retrial, even after he finished serving his prison sentence for killing Sue Wheelock. The government argued that given his past murder conviction and the evidence showing he killed Clementine and Karol, Monte posed a danger to the public and an obvious flight risk, given his history of escape and flight. Judge Hendrickson agreed, and imposed a high enough bond that Monte was unable to make bond. He was held in custody pending retrial, even though he had completed his prison sentence for killing Sue Wheelock. So, Monte wouldn't be free, at least yet, at least until he stood trial a second time for killing Clementine and Karol.

NINETEEN
MONTE'S RETRIAL

"The defendant wants to hide the truth because he's generally guilty. The defense attorney's job is to make sure the jury does not arrive at that truth."
– Alan Dershowitz

STARTING ON AUGUST 8, 2000, MONTE WAS TRIED once again for the Beavers' murders. By then, both Monte's biological and stepmothers had died. Monte's father had died in 1998. Monte's brother, Donnie, remained in prison. Monte hadn't had contact with his sister for decades. Monte faced retrial alone, as he had faced most trials in his life.

Judge Hendrickson was again assigned to preside over the new trial. Before the trial, Monte's attorneys renewed their motion for a change of venue. Given that Monte's

1998 trial just recently took place in Mount Pleasant, this time Judge Hendrickson agreed that Monte wouldn't likely receive a fair second trial in Mount Pleasant after all the publicity surrounding that trial. So, Judge Hendrickson granted the defense's change of venue motion. Judge Hendrickson ordered the second trial would be tried in Keokuk, Lee County, Iowa. Judge Hendrickson's home town.

For trial lawyers, there are few things worse than having to try the same case over again. Trials are like battles, or perhaps more like athletic games. For lawyers, preparing for trial takes a lot of work. It requires meeting with witnesses to review their expected testimony, identifying pieces of evidence to mark as exhibits, drafting, redrafting and redrafting again opening statements and closing arguments. Lawyers engage in strategic and tactical thinking and decision-making, piecing together how to try the case, determining what evidence to present in what order so as to maximize the persuasive effect, and in deciding what to say, and how to say it in the most persuasive manner possible when addressing the jury. And then during the trial itself, a trial attorney's adrenaline is pumping, reacting to unexpected developments as the case progresses, confronting witnesses, addressing the jurors. Trials involve preparation, perspiration, anticipation, and excitement.

Retrials, in contrast, are a letdown and a burden. You've been there, done that. It's hard to get excited to try the same case a second time around. You don't have the same sense of the unknown, of the unanticipated. I know. I've been there, and done that. During my career, I had to retry several cases for various reasons. It's not fun. So, as prosecutors Kivi and Riepe prepared to retry Monte a second time, to question the same witnesses a second time about the same things as last time, they struggled to get motivated. It was only the desire to see that justice was finally done, to give closure to the Beavers family, that provided Kivi and Riepe the necessary boost to see the case through another trial.

Monte's second trial lasted five days. It was a virtual repeat of the prior trial, with the same focus and same themes by both sides in opening statements and closing arguments. Only this time, the government would be extremely careful to make sure there wasn't the slightest reference to marijuana. The government's evidence was almost identical to the prior trial, other than this time the government left out references to Monte's marijuana grow. As in the first trial, Monte did not call any witnesses and didn't testify on his own behalf.

During the government's closing argument in the second trial, the government again focused on the forensic evidence. Twice, the prosecutor also commented on the failure of the defense to present a firearm expert to rebut the government's forensic ballistics evidence. The defense attorney objected both times, asserting it violated Monte's constitutional rights. Monte had the Fifth Amendment right to remain silent and had no burden of proof, so the defense had no obligation to rebut any of the government's evidence with its own expert. By suggesting otherwise, the prosecutor was improperly commenting on Monte's right to remain silent and shifting the burden of proof. Monte's attorneys moved for a mistrial each time. Judge Hendrickson denied the motions for a mistrial, but admonished the jury that the government had the burden of proof and that a criminal defendant had no such burden.

In the defense closing arguments, Monte's attorneys again attacked law enforcement officers on what they claimed was a sloppy investigation. The defense attorneys this time drilled down a little more, to emphasize even the smallest mistakes the government made in its investigation. They pointed out that the state's firearm expert forgot to record in his report anything about rifling marks left on the bullets that officers recovered from the poles that Monte and his brother used for target practice. The defense team pointed out how these marks were critical for the agent to later testify that the marks matched that of the bullet recovered from Clementine's head. Monte's attorneys also pointed out that five pieces of evidence, including palm prints from the murder scene and hair samples from Max Beavers, were labeled incorrectly in the evidence log. In the government's rebuttal closing argument, the prosecutor downplayed these as minor errors, arguing they were administrative in nature and didn't affect the investigation.

On August 17, 2000, after about only four hours of deliberations, this new jury found Monte guilty of first degree murder of both Clementine and Karol Beavers. Twice, now, a jury had found beyond a reasonable doubt that Monte had murdered Clementine and Karol. Between the two trials, 24 jurors had unanimously found Monte guilty. According to a newspaper report at the time, Monte again showed little emotion when Judge Hendrickson read the verdict.

This time around, there was no delay between the guilty verdicts and sentencing. Instead of several months' delay before imposition of sentence, Monte waived his right to have a separate sentencing hearing. So, after excusing the jury, Judge Hendrickson sentenced Monte on the spot. Like last time, Monte declined to speak at his own sentencing hearing. Judge Hendrickson once again sentenced Monte to two consecutive life sentences, and ordered him to pay $4,300 in restitution to Max Beavers for funeral costs. Monte was 39 years old.

About 20 members of the Beavers' extended family attended most of the five-day trial. Newspapers reported that when the judge read the first murder verdict, announcing that Monte was once again found guilty of murdering Clementine Beavers, there was a large sigh of relief among family members and tearful hugs. Max Beavers, then 77 years old, had attended only the first day of the retrial, and only attended long enough to testify. The emotional strain was simply too much for him to watch the whole trial. Randy Beavers, one of Max's sons, called Max from the courtroom to deliver news of the verdicts.

Monte's attorneys again appealed his conviction. This time, the attorneys focused primarily on what they alleged was an improper prosecution closing argument, specifically the reference to Monte not calling a firearms expert. Monte's attorneys claimed the government's closing argument shifted the burden of proof to Monte, in violation of his constitutional rights, because under the Fifth and Fourteenth Amendments a criminal defendant does not have the burden to produce any evidence. Monte had the right to remain silent meaning he didn't have to put on any evidence at all. To suggest otherwise, as the government did during closing argument, his attorneys reasoned, violated Monte's right to a fair trial. His attorneys also raised, once again, the unconstitutional April 1979 search and argued that all the ballistics evidence derived from that unlawful search should have been suppressed.

The Iowa Court of Appeals rejected the defense appeal. The Court of Appeals first found that the government's closing argument didn't focus on Monte's failure to testify, but rather, on the failure to produce a firearms expert. Thus, the government's argument didn't directly implicate Monte's right to remain silent. Further, the Court of Appeals found that the trial judge's sustaining of the defense objections and properly instructing the jury about the burden of proof was sufficient to remove any possible harm from the allegedly improper closing argument. Second, the Court of Appeals rejected Monte's request to revisit the admissibility of the evidence from the seizure of the firearm and ammunition. The court announced that the Iowa Supreme Court had already decided the issue about the admissibility of the firearm and ballistics evidence and the court wasn't going to reverse its own ruling on that matter.

Monte's appeal was over. He lost. He stood convicted of two first degree murders. Monte would spend the rest of his life in prison.

TWENTY
EPILOGUE

"Whoever fights monsters should see to it that in the process he does not become a monster. And if you gaze long enough into an abyss, the abyss will gaze back into you." — Friedrich Nietzsche

THE BEAVERS FAMILY SUFFERED GREATLY throughout the decades between the 1978 murders and Monte's ultimate conviction and life sentences in 2000. Max, in particular, suffered the most. He had to testify multiple times, reliving the horror of discovering his slain wife and daughter over and over again. Max had to endure suspicion and direct accusations that he killed his wife and daughter. He also bore the weight of blaming himself for failing to protect his wife and daughter that awful night.

In the aftermath of the criminal prosecution, many of the Beavers family members harbored hard feelings against the attorneys who defended Monte in the trials and on appeal. Ethically, attorneys have a duty to zealously represent their clients. Particularly in criminal cases, defense attorneys are required by the Sixth Amendment to the United States Constitution to provide adequate representation of their clients. Defense attorneys are not concerned with justice; that isn't their job. Their responsibility is to defend someone accused of criminal conduct by all ethical means at their disposal. This is their responsibility even if they believe their clients are guilty, even if they detest their clients, even if they think their clients are monsters.

For the criminal justice system to work, for it to protect the liberties of all the people against the power of the government, it must be difficult to convict any one person of a crime. The system must be robust and the burden of proof high. Defense attorneys should endeavor to throw up roadblocks against conviction and, in particular in the American system, ensure that the government uses only constitutional means to convict a person of a crime. This may mean that some guilty people go free. That is the cost of a free society. Eminent English jurist William Blackstone best articulated this principle in the 1760s, now known as Blackstone's ratio or Blackstone's formulation: "It is better that ten persons escape than that one innocent suffer."[1]

Intellectually, a person can appreciate and accept this

---

1. William Blackstone, *Commentaries on the Laws of England* (1765). That principle was embraced, if not expanded, in America. Benjamin Franklin increased the ratio, saying: "it is better 100 guilty Persons should escape than that one innocent Person should suffer." Benjamin

concept. When one thinks dispassionately about the criminal justice system, it is understandable that for the system to work, for us to ensure that it is extremely difficult for an innocent person to be convicted, criminal defense attorneys must make every challenge they can, and argue every reasonable doubt that they can imagine, to set their clients free.

But victims aren't dispassionate. Victims understandably don't care much about the system as a whole. They care about the crime that victimized them. Particularly in murder cases and other violent crimes when victims and their family members have suffered a horrendous loss, a criminal trial isn't an intellectual exercise. To the victims in these cases, the broader principles involved in maintaining a free society through a robust criminal justice system are not their priorities. Victims want justice. In many cases, victims desire vengeance. From their perspective, the machinations of conniving defense attorneys to seize upon perceived technicalities in the law are unjust efforts to stand in the way of and interfere with the administration of justice.

Thus, it was understandable that Max, his children, and his children's children, were frustrated and upset with Monte's defense attorneys. The Beavers family are fair and just and compassionate people, and they understood at a fundamental level that the defense attorneys were simply doing their jobs. But that doesn't mean they had to like it.

Franklin, *Works* 293 (1970), Letter from Benjamin Franklin to Benjamin Vaughan (14 March 1785).

It doesn't mean that it was easy for them to watch and listen to attempts to vilify Max or distract jurors from the evidence of Monte's guilt.

Most of the Beavers family members sat through both of Monte's trials. After the verdict in the second and final trial, Max's son Randy Beavers, then 50 years old, spoke to the press on behalf of the family. The *Mount Pleasant News* quoted him.

"Once it went to the jury, you can't anticipate what they will do," he said, his eyes brimming with tears. "We'd like to pass on our appreciation to the jury. My dad is certainly pleased justice was done a second time," he said, adding the emotional strain on his father was too much for him to sit through the entire proceeding. "He has his days," Randy Beavers said. "Sometimes emotions overcome him. There isn't a day go by that he doesn't think about it."

MANY OF THE FAMILY MEMBERS, INCLUDING MAX, submitted written victim impact statements to the court. There were fourteen written victim impact statements in all, written by Max and by the victims' children, brothers, sisters, cousins, uncles, nieces, grandchildren. Victim impact statements are almost always emotionally taxing to read, particularly in a murder case. Victim impact statements provide a glimpse, but only a glimpse, of the immense pain and loss the family members have suffered, and reflect the mental and emotional struggles they have experienced, and continued to experience, even decades after the murders.

The written victim impact statements in the Beavers' murder case reflect that the surviving family members were understandably frustrated with a criminal justice system that suppressed evidence, dismissed charges, and then overturned Monte's conviction after the first trial. They were upset that it took two decades to ultimately hold Monte accountable for his crimes. After the trial, Randy Beavers explained to the press: "We thought the rightful murderer was behind bars. They [the appellate courts] wield their decision from a law standpoint, not from the victims' families' standpoint. I don't even think they considered if it [the reference to marijuana that caused a new trial] biased the jury." The family members viewed the various legal machinations surrounding Monte's prosecution as legal technicalities arising from a justice system tailored to protect criminals at the cost of victims. It is easy to appreciate how crime victims find it hard to embrace a justice system that struggles to provide a just process for everyone, though it may not result in a just outcome every time.

The written victim impact statements also expressed appreciation for the efforts made by the agents and prosecutors. Many of the family members expressed deep gratitude for the continued dedication of law enforcement officers and prosecutors who doggedly pursued the case, despite the legal setbacks.

Most of the family members' victim impact statements also reflected a loss of trust they had in others, and in their own safety. They were no longer trusting of others as they had been in the past. They could no longer feel safe in their homes. They became paranoid about their own safety and overprotective of their children. Even two decades after the murders, the surviving family members remained vigilant, apprehensive, untrusting.

Although the Beavers were a Catholic family, and Catholic doctrine is against the death penalty, the family members' victim impact statements revealed that many of them wished Monte would have been executed. These family members struggled with the conflict between their religion and the death penalty. It was Monte's complete lack of remorse, in their view, that justified the extreme punishment of death for him. I can't imagine the internal mental stress that it must cause crime victims when their emotions and personal sense of justice conflict with their very personal religious beliefs that dictate forgiveness and the preservation of life under any circumstances. The senselessness of the murders also made some of the family members doubt their faith, made them question how a loving God could allow such evil to occur.

One victim impact statement in particular, written by a grandchild and niece of the victims, was viscerally impactful. This family member was only four years old at the time of the murders, but was in her early 20s by the time of the second trial. Her letter had a couple parts to it, one addressed to the sentencing judge, another to Monte. Here is a portion of her victim impact statement, the portion directed to Monte Seager, which she read out loud at Monte's sentencing hearing.

. . .

MONTE SEAGER, MY LETTER TO YOU

For twenty years I have primed myself for the moment I would get a chance to speak to you about what you did to my family in open court. Now that I think about it, I think God was just letting this case ride for twenty years so I would get this chance.

If someone would ask me, "who is the one person you hate the most?" I would answer that question without even giving it a second thought. It is you. I have hated you for as long as I can remember. Your name was probably one of the first names I memorized outside my family. That isn't a compliment either. What makes me the most mad, is that you were the last person my aunt saw that night. And you are the only person alive that knows what happened exactly that night.

There was a point a few years ago that I wanted to see you in person, sit down face to face and see what you looked like. I had seen the pictures in the paper but it just wasn't the same. I went as far as to call the prison to see about visiting. I wanted you to know who I was and what I have vowed to spend my life doing. I will make sure that your last breath is spent breathing in recycled prison air.

I was given the opportunity to visit your prison last year in one of my criminology classes. I decided not to go. I didn't want to see the condition of the prison.... [C]an you really blame me for wishing the worst for you?

The one question I have for you isn't the one you are probably thinking I would ask. I'm not going to ask why. Instead, *my question to you is why do it and not stand up for it? You decided to take the lives of my grandma and aunt from my family and the world, what kind of man are you to not admit you did it? I think it shows that you are weak. You may think you are some God like man with the power to kill, but you're not, you can't stand up for the work you do. What is the point of you using good air that my grandma and aunt could be using? If the State of Iowa had the death penalty, you'd better believe I would have a front row seat. I would want to be the last person you saw before you died. I would want to see the terror in your eyes as you know your life is about to end, tick, tock, tick, tock. But, Iowa doesn't have the death penalty. So, in consolation, I get to know seconds, minutes, hours, days, weeks, months, and years get taken from your life one second at a time, behind bars.*

I used to think the reason the case didn't come around until now was because our legal system was worthless. That isn't the case, because, Monte, God wanted you to think you were home free and you would be getting out in a year. It didn't work out the way you wanted did it? It is funny how God turns things around. You messed with His world, now He is messing with yours.

… niece that was in the house the same day you were. It was my finger prints that were found in the kitchen and it was my blonde hair found on Karol's jeans. A part of me was there when you killed them both. And since I have to live with that, you can spend the rest of your life in prison knowing that I am out here and I won't allow you to ever breath[e] free air again. My name is _____ and I am one of

your other victims you never knew you had.[2]

CARRYING THROUGH ALL OF THE VICTIM IMPACT statements, however, was an overriding, recurring question. Why? Why did Monte do this? Why did he shoot a middle-aged woman in cold blood? Why did he target Karol? Why did he kill her? Why rape her as she was dying?

That is the same question everyone in the community asked at the time, and continues to ask. There was speculation at the time that Karol was involved romantically with Monte, or had spurned his advances, or was involved in Monte's drug world. There was speculation that Max was somehow involved, or that someone was angry with Max and took it out on his family. The investigation and prosecution put all these speculations to rest. There was nothing to any of the rumors. Which left everyone, including the Beavers family, with the same unanswered question. Then why?

Monte never testified at his trials. He never spoke at the sentencing hearings. He didn't answer that question for them at the time. Until now, he has never really told anyone what he was thinking at the time, why he did what he did.

The truth of why Monte killed is likely much more

---

2. The ellipses mark portions of the victim impact statement in the court file that were unreadable. I have also omitted the name to preserve the victim's privacy.

unsettling and unsatisfactory. The truth is that there is evil in the world, and that humans can be inhumane. In my many years working as a prosecutor and judge, I have dealt on occasion with psychopaths, people who lack the ability to feel empathy for others, who are incapable of feeling the natural human emotion of sympathy or care for others. These people, almost always men, are missing an essential part of what makes us human: the inherent ability to imagine what others feel, and the desire to save others from suffering. Psychopaths are indifferent to human suffering. It means nothing to them. The pain and suffering of others triggers no emotional reaction in them. It has been my experience that the degree to which this human quality is missing from some humans varies. I have dealt with several men in my time who seemed to have no empathy at all, who could see another human being suffering and have no human emotional response whatso-ever. Monte is one of them.

When I spoke to Monte in prison nearly 50 years after he committed the murders, while researching this book, Monte confessed to me that he did, in fact, murder Clementine and Karol. But he told me that the brutal murders he committed were just something that happened. He claimed it wasn't part of a plan, that he felt the events just rolled on, somehow out of his control. As if he were not really responsible for his actions. As if he were as much a victim of fate as Clementine and Karol. From his perspective, the murders just happened as if he was a passive player in the tragic events.

Monte's version of the murders he provided me when I

interviewed him in prison minimized his premeditation and planning, and by extension, his culpability for the monstrous acts. Monte told me that he was in McMillan Park that evening shooting out street lights for entertainment when, on his way home, he just happened upon Karol's house and decided on the spur of the moment to kidnap her. He explained that when he snuck into the Beavers' home, he heard the TV on downstairs and decided to "eliminate that obstacle" to carrying out his plan of kidnapping Karol. He told me that after he shot Clementine, he had decided just to leave the home, but when he came back upstairs he ran into Karol. He claimed to me that the first time he shot Karol was simply an accident. He claimed the gun just went off. Once he shot her and she was down on the ground, though, Monte shot Karol the second time, in the back of her head, he told me, "to put her out of her misery." He told me that he then went outside the house and sat down under a tree for a while trying to understand what just happened. Eventually, he got up, went back in the house, dragged Karol into the garage, and raped her. He told me he didn't know why he did it. Told me that it felt like he was in a car without brakes or steering.

When telling me how he shot Clementine in the back of the head while she sat in her rocking chair watching TV on a peaceful Sunday night, Monte didn't display the slightest degree of sympathy or regret or remorse. He told me about shooting this innocent woman in the same manner and with the same tone and facial expression that he told me about how he shot out street lights. It meant just as much, or as little, to him. When Monte told me of how he shot Karol, twice, and dragged her unconscious body into the garage, when he told me of how he raped her as she lay dying, I detected no sympathy or empathy, no remorse, no feelings in his facial expressions, and heard none in the tone of his voice. When he described what he did to Karol in the garage, Monte looked me straight in the eyes and coldly, if grudgingly, told me that he couldn't exactly call it making love to Karol. Shooting her, violently raping her as she lay dying on a cold garage floor, was, to Monte, just something he did. Her suffering, what she was feeling, meant nothing to him. When Monte told me of beating Sue Wheelock to death, his explanation was that he "guessed" he hit her a few too many times. That he crushed in her skull by repeatedly striking her with heavy glass bottles, that the pain she felt must have been excruciating, were of little note or concern to Monte.

So that is the unsatisfying answer to the question why. Sometimes evil people do evil things. Sometimes there are monsters in this world. Sometimes horribly bad things happen to wonderfully good people. And those victims did nothing to bring on the violence, did nothing wrong, were not at fault in any way for what happened to them. The blunt and troubling truth is, it could happen to you, as it could happen to me, as it happened to them.

After the murder trials, Max Beavers carried on as best he could for his remaining years. He struggled every October 29 on the anniversary of the deaths of Clementine and Karol, just as the rest of the family continue to do today. Max was hospitalized on October 29, 2016, suffering from sepsis in his lungs. He never left the hospital. Max Beavers died at the age of 95 on November 6, 2016, a little more than 38 years after Monte Seager slaughtered Max's wife and daughter. Max now rests next to Clementine and Karol in the Catholic cemetery in Mount Pleasant.

Beavers gravestone (photo by author)

Sue Wheelock rests in peace not far from the Beavers, in the cemetery on the other side of the road. She isn't buried in a family plot; no other family members are buried nearby. Her parents passed long ago, and are buried elsewhere, as are the grandparents who raised her. Somewhere else in the same cemetery lie the remains of Sue's father's first wife, a woman who died only a few months after Sue was born. They remain connected, yet distant, in death as they were in life.

Sue Wheelock's gravestone (photo by author)

Monte Seager, now in his mid-sixties, remains in custody, serving two consecutive life sentences without parole at the Anamosa State Penitentiary. The prison is located in Anamosa, Iowa, only about 20 miles from my judicial chambers. Beginning in 1872, over a period of about 30 years, prison labor constructed the buildings and the prison's six-feet wide, 22-feet tall walls out of dolomite limestone. The prison resembles a castle. It is an imposing structure, the only one Monte will likely ever see.

Monte now has long white hair which he wears tied back in a pony tail. He is slope-shouldered, sports a bushy white beard, and carries a small potbelly. He looks not unlike Santa Claus, or perhaps an aging rock band groupie. When we talked during my visits in the Anamosa prison, he was soft-spoken, quiet, and calm. He looks and acts very little like the violent, heartless young man he was nearly 50 years ago. But for his cold brown eyes, which remain the same, it's difficult to imagine him capable of the atrocities he committed.

Monte lives alone in a one-man cell. He has worked at various times in the kitchen, sometimes as an orderly in the prison's medical facility, but spends most of his time watching television and reading. He has had very few visitors over the decades since his convictions. He was once disciplined for using a computer to disseminate a sexual joke in violation of the rules for computer use, but otherwise seems to have largely complied with the rules and regulations governing his existence. He has become, it seems, acclimated to prison life.

And the truth is that Monte will never be set free. The time for appeals and post-conviction litigation has long since passed. And now that he has confessed the murders to me, he will never be able to claim innocence. Monte will die alone in prison.

ACKNOWLEDGMENTS

In researching and writing a book like this, I benefitted from the assistance of many, and imposed on them all, taking their time and dredging up memories that many would have likely preferred to remain buried in the recesses of their minds. I apologize to those whom I have wounded by reviving the memories of these horrific events.

I owe a debt of gratitude to many people for their assistance and guidance in bringing this book into being. I credit Wendy Christian with encouraging me to write this book, something I had toyed with doing for years and might never have accomplished without her prompting me to do so. Several of my close friends patiently listened to me talk about my research and politely read through early drafts of this manuscript, providing me with sound suggestions and corrections. These friends include Wendy, Sean Berry, Pete Deegan, Rich Murphy, Sali Van Weelden, and Claudia Streeter. I thank them for their candid feedback which made this book much better.

I also appreciate the memories of Karol my big brother, Dave, shared with me, and his feedback on a draft of the manuscript.

I am indebted to John Paine for his editorial services; his frank and insightful feedback made this a better book. And I sincerely thank Leya and Steven Booth with Genius Books & Media, Inc. for believing in this project and seeing it through to completion.

Pat White, Director of the Henry County History Center, was wonderfully helpful in assisting me in looking up old newspaper articles, thumbing through past Mount Pleasant High School yearbooks, and in otherwise mining the Center's archives for information about the Beavers' and Wheelock murders.

Mount Pleasant Chief of Police, Lyle Murray, was extremely accommodating in giving me access to the investigation file and evidence from the Beavers' murder cases. And I deeply appreciate my old friend, Brad Gillis, who spent a couple hours with me one cold afternoon in January opening dusty old boxes and envelopes as we perused the evidence from the Beavers' murder case. Likewise, I am thankful to the clerk of court personnel in Henry, Lee, and Des Moines counties, the Henry County Attorney's Office, and the Henry County and Des Moines County sheriffs' offices for making the court files available to me.

I also want to thank Gus Hagers for his willingness to share with me his memories of the investigation and his efforts to solve the crimes. I'm equally appreciative that Terry Duncan answered my call made out of the blue and was willing to recount to me the terror of the night he bravely entered the Beavers' home alone, even though he was convinced the killer remained inside. Likewise, I appreciate the time that Jim Kivi and Ron Mower spent speaking to me on the phone and sharing their memories with me.

I am thankful too, to my former boss, Dave Heaton, for relating his memories of Sue Wheelock and the horror of the day he found his valued employee in a pool of blood on the floor of his restaurant, and to his wife, Carmen, for sharing her memories of Sue with me. Likewise, I appreciate the time that my former coworkers, including Charlie Vestweber, took to provide me with their recollections of Monte Seager and Sue Wheelock.

I was able to track down only one distant relative of Monte Seager to learn about his family history and I thank her for her wiliness to share what she knew about a member of her family that cast a shadow over an otherwise quality family line.

Many of Karol's former friends and classmates took time out of their busy lives to tell me more about the wonderful girl they knew and loved. I am thankful for their time and for sharing their memories with me. I hope I have used their words about her to reflect in this book at least some of the radiance of Karol's kind soul.

I am most deeply grateful to many of the members of the Beavers family for their willingness to talk with me and share their memories of their beloved Clementine and Karol; I am sorry if my dredging up these tragic events saddened them. I sincerely hope that I have translated their loving memories of Clementine and Karol in the book to help shed the label of crime victims and clothe them again with the vibrant personalities that filled their lives.

I also must acknowledge that Monte Seager was willing to talk with me, and to confess the murders, and thus put to rest any lingering doubts as to who committed them.

Made in the USA
Columbia, SC
06 May 2025

57612603R00174